PICTURE HISTORY OF THE CUNARD LINE, 1840–1990

FRANK O. BRAYNARD
AND
WILLIAM H. MILLER, JR.

DOVER PUBLICATIONS, INC.
New York

for David Edwardsen

beloved friend, splendid artist and
yet another fan of the Cunarders

ACKNOWLEDGMENTS

Many hands have assisted in creating this book, but the authors wish to extend very special appreciation to Everett Viez, master maritime photographer and collector. Without his extensive support, cooperation and generosity, this book might not have been possible. Special thanks also go to Frank Duffy, public relations director at Moran Towing & Transportation Company, who shared many outstanding photographs from Moran's master files. Furthermore, a group of very kind "liner friends" has given invaluable help: Jim Cavanagh, F. Leonard Jackson, Brenton Jenkins, Michael D.

J. Lennon, Jan Loeff, Abe Michaelson, Richard K. Morse, Fred Rodriguez, Victor Scrivens, James L. Shaw, Michael Shernoff, Peter Smith, Willie and Marie Tinnemeyer and Steffen Weirauch. Further kind assistance came from the Cunard Line, Flying Camera, Inc., Hotel Queen Mary, South China Morning Post, Ltd., Southern Newspapers, Ltd. and the World Ship Society Photo Library. And, of course, our deepest appreciation to our families and to the staff of Dover Publications, Inc.

Published in Canada by General Publishing Company, Ltd.,
30 Lesmill Road, Don Mills, Toronto, Ontario.
Published in the United Kingdom by Constable and Company, Ltd.,
3 The Lanchesters, 162–164 Fulham Palace Road, London W6 9ER.

Picture History of the Cunard Line, 1840–1990 is a new work, first
published by Dover Publications, Inc., in 1991.

Manufactured in the United States of America
Dover Publications, Inc.
31 East 2nd Street
Mineola, N.Y. 11501

Library of Congress Cataloging-in-Publication Data

Braynard, Frank Osborn, 1916–
Picture history of the Cunard Line, 1840–1990 / by Frank O.
Braynard and William H. Miller.
p.   cm.
Includes bibliographical references (p.   ) and index.
ISBN 0-486-26550-1 (pbk.)
1. Cunard Steamship Company, Ltd.—History—Pictorial works.
I. Miller, William H., 1948– . II. Title.
HE945.C9B73   1991
387.5′06′541—dc20
90-47959
CIP

CONTENTS

SOURCES AND PHOTOGRAPHERS

Aerial Explorations, Inc.: 45 (bottom).
Frank O. Braynard Collection: 3–7,9, 11, 13 (bottom), 26 (top), 33,
    35, 37, 41 (top), 42 (bottom), 45 (top), 46, 47, 48 (top), 49
    (bottom), 50 (bottom), 51, 70, 73–76, 77 (bottom), 78 (left), 81
    (top), 84, 86–92, 95, 100, 106, 108 (bottom), 111 (top), 116
    (bottom), 119 (top).
Alexander Brown: 120.
Jim Cavanagh: 99.
Robert E. Coates: 26 (top), 42 (bottom), 46 (top).
Cunard Line: 126 (bottom, left and right), 128–132.
Flying Camera, Inc.: 110, 111 (bottom), 126 (top).
Frank: 76.
Alexander Gmelin (courtesy of Stephan Gmelin): 42 (top), 53
    (bottom), 58, 61.
Leo J. Heffernan: 106 (bottom).
C. R. Hoffmann: 20 (top), 107.
Hotel Queen Mary: 119 (bottom).
F. Leonard Jackson: 113 (bottom).
Brenton Jenkins Collection: 104.
Michael D. J. Lennon: 108 (top).
Owin Levi: 45 (top).
Edwin Levick: 16, 50 (bottom).
Jan Loeff: 39.
Moran Towing & Transportation Co.: 96, 98, 120, 124/125.
Richard K. Morse Collection: 48 (bottom).
J. Fred Rodriguez: 118, 122.
Morris Rosenfeld: 106 (top).
R. Scozzafava: 48 (bottom).
Victor Scrivens Collection: 25 (top).
James L. Shaw: 121 (bottom).
T. Sheehan: 119 (top).
Peter Smith Collection: 112.
South China Morning Post, Ltd.: 121 (top).
Southern Newspapers PLC: 105, 127.
Steamship Historical Society Collection, University of Baltimore
    Library: 63.
Steffen: 11.
Willie Tinnemeyer: 20, 60 (bottom), 81 (bottom), 82 (top), 83, 101,
    107, 115.
Everett Viez Collection: 8, 10, 12, 13 (top), 15–19, 21–24, 25 (bottom),
    26 (bottom), 27–32, 34, 36, 38, 40, 41 (bottom), 42 (top), 45
    (bottom), 49 (top), 50 (top), 53–56, 58, 59, 60 (top), 61–69, 71, 77
    (top), 78 (right), 79, 80, 82 (bottom), 85, 93, 97, 102, 103, 109,
    110, 114, 116 (top), 117.
Steffen Weirauch Collection: 52, 113 (top).
World Ship Society Photo Library: 44.

FOREWORD

OVER THE PAST 150 years "the Cunard" has achieved a reputation and history that have become legendary.

In the annals of passenger shipping where (in this century especially) luxury, safety and reliability have come to be the accepted norm of ocean travel, Cunard has often been the yardstick by which all other shipping companies on the highly competitive North Atlantic run have been measured: a hallmark of excellence for others to emulate.

From a century and a half ago, when Samuel Cunard realized his ambition of creating the first regular passenger-and-mail steamship service (which has also become the last to cross the Atlantic), to the present day of luxurious cruise ships, a host of vessels have been the tools by which the company has achieved its prosperity and fame.

From the early wooden paddle steamers that rhythmically beat their way across the vast expanse of an almost empty Atlantic to innovative ships that introduced, among other things, electric light to ocean travel; from humble cargo ships to the world's mightiest—and often fastest—passenger liners, the changing fleet of the Cunard has always attracted attention and worldwide acclaim, in war as well as in peace. Many of the line's ships have over the years commanded fierce loyalties and, on their passing, national mourning.

The great liners were an everyday spectacle, one that was often taken for granted, when I was a schoolboy receiving my education in Cowes on the Isle of Wight. Five or six liners passed through the confines of the Solent almost every day as they arrived at or departed from Southampton (just a few miles to the north) and I soon became interested in these massive, moving creations of man.

I kept a weekly sailing list in my school desk, hoping to catch a glimpse of an old favorite or a new arrival through my classroom window. I would also walk home along the shore road in the late afternoon with the hope of seeing, perhaps, the *Caronia*, beautifully lit by the late afternoon sun, or the *Queen Mary* steaming gloriously toward Southampton, the setting sun sharply contrasting her black hull against her white superstructure, red funnels and the pale blues of sea and sky. On one such remembered occasion, each rivet head, caught by the sun, glistened in bright highlight.

Sighting a Cunard ship never ceased to thrill, especially at night, when every porthole, every window, lit by a soft, pre-neon yellow light, reflected toward me on the ship's black, oily wash.

And those funnels! Lit up in the darkness, they were especially magnificent—a bright, glowing red from which issued pale gray plumes of smoke illuminated from underneath by the glow of the ship's lights.

Yes, Cunard was my favorite and those who sailed its ships my heroes. As an enthusiastic "spotter," I soon became interested in the history of what I saw and, in later years, attempted to repay my hobby for the great pleasure that I had derived from it: by writing *Transatlantic Liners at War: The Story of the Queens; Queen Mary: 50 Years of Splendour; Titanic: 75 Years of Legend; Queen Elizabeth 2: A Ship for all Seasons;* and *Queen Elizabeth: From Victory to Valhalla.*

So it is with great pleasure that I now introduce *Picture History of the Cunard Line, 1840–1990* by Frank Braynard and William Miller, ship buffs and ship authors par excellence.

This fine album of photographs of Cunard ships will surely add another sequin to the dazzling history that is Cunard's.

DAVID F. HUTCHINGS
Lee-on-the-Solent
England

PREFACES

I BEGAN COLLECTING LINER ARTIFACTS, framed prints, paintings, brochures, news clips, sailing schedules, rate sheets and other ephemera and memorabilia when I was five or six years old. By the time I was seven, I could spell "Leviathan" (the name of a great ship) although I could not spell my own name. This hobby has turned into my lifetime work—and no company has given me more joy or satisfaction than the Cunard Line. Few people have been as fortunate as I have in having lifetime careers that run right down center line with a hobby. Bill Miller is also lucky enough to be on the way of turning his avocation into a full-time profession.

When I was in the fifth grade at Friends Academy, my interest in liners led me to do a paper on the history of great passenger ships. Miss Otterson, my teacher, encouraged me to submit documentation and, along with the essay, I turned in a Cunard folder containing fine colored pictures of outstanding Cunard liners and stories about them. I got a good grade but, to my horror, my teacher casually let me know that she had lost my brochure. You can imagine my joy forty or fifty years later when someone gave me a second copy of this choice, beautiful folder—something that had meant so much in my youth. I guard it with a passion from all Miss Ottersons!

Years later, William North and I decided to do a book on the early Cunard paddle wheelers. North, a Cunard vice president and manager of its public relations department, had made an excellent start on the work. Generously, he turned his files over to me and I continued to gather engravings and information. Bill went on to a new career as director of public affairs for Mystic Seaport, Mystic, Connecticut. For the Cunard project, I hoped to visit England and dig up little-known facts about these early Cunarders—such as information about the cow that sailed aboard the *Britannia*, the very first Cunarder (1840). There may yet be a copy of an obscure country newspaper that mentions the name of the farmer who sold this cow to Samuel Cunard. I also wanted to find under what circumstances that marvelous "Boston Mails" china, which featured interior views of the first Cunard quartet of liners, was issued in 1841. My sister Margaret married Arthur Peabody, whose family possessed a huge assortment of this china, executed in old lavender. Was it used aboard these early side-wheel steamers, or was it issued to commemorate their new service? I never really solved these mysteries, but over the years such questions have given Cunard a very special place in my mind.

Bill Miller and I wish to thank Dover Publications for giving us the opportunity to do this picture book—to have the chance to show some of our favorite photos of some of the greatest (and even some of the lesser) Cunard beauties and to share with others our personal enthusiasm for the Cunard traditions and history. As the most famous ocean-liner company of all time, Cunard is certainly a splendid subject about

which to build this book—and here's to Cunard in their second 150 years of contribution to shipping and good will between peoples.

FRANK O. BRAYNARD

In the 1950s, my love affair with ocean liners blossomed and the Cunard fleet quickly became one of my favorites. We were practically neighbors. The Cunarders sailed frequently from New York then, often three or four times a week. On their trips down the Hudson, they would glide majestically past my home in Hoboken, framed by the spectacular Manhattan skyline. There were indelible impressions of each—the *Queen Mary* in clear winter sunlight, the *Britannic* in fading afternoon shadows, the *Sylvania* in fog. I would have a few all-too-brief moments to study them: the position of their funnels, the pristine all-white superstructures, the form of their long hulls. Often, I would return home quickly and attempt to sketch them, always using ink and rulers. I would try to recall details: The *Queen Elizabeth* had more rake to her bow than the *Queen Mary*, the *Mary* had one extra black band on her forward funnel (three bands in all) and the *Mauretania* had extra lifeboats aft. What great fun! I probably had more drawings of Cunarders (the very names conjure up images of magically romantic ships) than any others. Now, Frank Braynard and I have the good fortune to put together this book, with fascinating photographs taking the place of those earlier drawings, which were not continued beyond childhood.

In the early sixties, I would often cross the Hudson on the Lackawanna ferries for a visit to "Steamship Row," that great collection of shipping offices in lower Manhattan. Cunard's headquarters had a special place on my list. Certainly, it was the most spectacular—an enormous, vaulted space, a mosaic ceiling, a vast rotunda lined with mahogany desks and one of the finest model collections anywhere. These miniature recreations rested in glass-encased splendor—the Queens and the *Majestic*, a white-hulled "first" *Mauretania* and, in rear alcoves, the *Berengaria*, the twin-stack freighter *Alsatia* and the second, "new" *Mauretania*. Once, a friend and I had a very special treat. Invited down to the labyrinth of basement supply and storerooms, we were given a large collection of the oversize posters and prints that were so typical of those years of ocean travel. (Ironically, the brisk, ever-expanding liner-memorabilia market pays upward of $500 for the simplest of these framable prints.)

In later years, I included Cunarders in almost all of the books that I wrote, always seeking fresh, unpublished views and the enlightening anecdote and detailed recollection. The Cunard liners, usually the three Queens, appeared on no less than eight dustjackets. Their appeal seems undiminished, and so Frank Braynard and I embarked on this project, a grand tour of sorts, mostly in nostalgia, of one of the greatest fleets ever to sail on any sea. Perhaps, they were, in fact, the very greatest of all. We gathered most of the photographs from Frank's basement "vaults" and from Everett Viez' spectacular collection in southern Florida. Together, these represent the finest ocean liner photograph archives in private hands.

This book was prompted by Cunard's sesquicentennial, an anniversary marked in 1990 by celebratory crossings and cruises, books and commemorative exhibitions. In New York, the Ocean Liner Museum organized "Cunard—150 Transatlantic Years" at the Forbes Building on lower Fifth Avenue.

Selecting items must have been quite difficult, considering the company's extraordinary history, its enormous fleet (from paddlers to four-stackers to Sea Goddess yachts) and its mammoth output of literature, such as sailing lists, deck plans and other printed materials. Inevitably, some of these baggage tags and menu cards were on display and, along with models, posters, china and silver and that most popular of collectibles, the ashtray. It was a glorious tribute to a glorious fleet. We hope that this book adds something as well. It is a grand review—the *Britannia* and the *Persia*, the *Campania* and the *Lusitania*, *Olympic* and *Georgic*, *Caronia*, *Carmania*, *Vistafjord* and, of course, the three Queens. You can almost hear the whistles sounding. Happy birthday, Cunard!

WILLIAM H. MILLER, JR.

SOME EARLY CUNARDERS:
1840–1905

THE USE OF STEAM power on steamboats was one thing, its use on oceangoing ships was quite a different matter. All the earliest experiments clearly indicate that Robert Fulton and the other early inventors intended to use the power of steam in harbors and on rivers only. It was not until Captain Moses Rogers and the 300-ton *Savannah* in 1819 that anyone really tried to use steam on a ship. The articles of incorporation of the Savannah Steam Ship Company stated that its goal was to determine whether it was feasible to apply the power of steam in navigating the oceans of the world. And that is exactly what the *Savannah* did prove on her voyage from Savannah, Georgia, to Liverpool, Copenhagen, Stockholm and St. Petersburg. England was quick to learn the lesson of the 99-foot-long *Savannah*, with her swivel smokestack and collapsible paddle wheels, and Channel steamers soon were linking ports in England with the Continent, clearly foretelling steam's conquest of the Atlantic itself. There were still many problems to be solved. Early steamships had to use salt water in their boilers, which meant that after a few hours of steaming they would have to stop, let the engines cool off and send men inside the boilers to chip off the salt that had caked on the inside. The boilers themselves were a serious problem in early steamships. It was some time before they could be made really tight. Early steam pressure had to be low because of the constant danger of explosion; pressure of more than a few pounds per square inch was risky. Some early steamer arrangements had a boiler on one ship and the passengers on another, tied to the power unit but separate. Boiler explosions and fires were common.

Transatlantic passenger service began on a regular basis in 1838 with the *Great Western*. She was built by Isambard Kingdom Brunel, that amazing bridge builder, engineer and pioneer. Steam pressure was only five pounds per square inch, but she boasted 750 horsepower and could make a top speed of 11 knots. Just before the new Brunel masterpiece was to sail, a little Channel steamer—the *Sirius*—appeared and, to everyone's surprise, headed across the ocean toward New York. It was a race, the start of the Blue Ribbon, and *Sirius* won. But she did not remain long in the field. *Great Western* started it all, making seventy transatlantic crossings between 1838 and 1844. Meanwhile, on July 4, 1840, Samuel Cunard, Canadian shipowner and a man with spirit, sailed aboard his *Britannia* on her first trip from Liverpool. This was the beginning of the Cunard Line.

Cunard had been born in November 1787. A Canadian whose father had come from Philadelphia, he spend most of his early life at Halifax and quickly became infatuated with ships and shipping. When his father retired from the family's small sailing-ship firm, he took over as head and soon renamed it Samuel Cunard & Company. Although he eventually expanded the business to 40 sailing vessels by 1838, he saw great potential in the new maritime technology—steam. He felt that steamships could be proven safe and reliable, and that they could be made profitable. Lacking sufficient support in Nova Scotia, he traveled to London in January 1839 and proposed that "steam boats" carry the government's mail across the North Atlantic. While there were other contenders for this prized contract, he finally succeeded. The agreement between the Admiralty and Cunard was signed on May 4. Remuneration was fixed at £55,000 a year for a regular service that was to begin on June 4, 1840 and run for at least seven years. The company, named the British & North American Royal Mail Steam Packet Company, soon became commonly known as the Cunard Line and sometimes as "Mr. Cunard's Line."

Samuel Cunard could not have been happier as his company grew steadily. For his great help during the Crimean War (1853–56), for which Cunard provided a veritable armada of liner-troopships, Cunard was rewarded with a baronetcy. Sir Samuel died on April 28, 1865.

BRITANNIA (above; opposite, top).

The *Britannia* was fully rigged with square sails, which were used often. Her power plant was a two-cylinder, side-lever steam engine; she could make 8.5 knots. Her engine was the work of R. Napier and Co., on the Clyde, Scotland. She burned 38 tons of coal a day and, on her first trip, took 12 days and ten hours to reach Halifax from Liverpool. Her terminal port in the United States was Boston. The steam pressure of the *Britannia*'s engine "would hardly lift the lid off a teapot." It was only five pounds PSI (per square inch) but, with the help of sails and the wind, the ship managed to make eight knots, and she could move ahead even when there was no wind. That was the great difference, and the reason that sail was doomed on the oceans of the world. But for the moment, the *Britannia* looked every inch a sailing ship. She had the traditional clipper bow, three tall masts, a figurehead and gilded decorations around her squared-off stern. True, she had two huge enclosed paddle wheels (28' in diameter), one on either side amidships, and a straight smokestack. It was colored a bright orange-red, had a thick black band at the very top and two thin black bands evenly dividing the lower portion into three parts. Her paddle boxes had space on top on which an officer could walk. This was the beginning of the bridge and pilot house. Captain Henry Woodruff was master and his chief engineer was Peter Kenneth. The ship's total complement was 89. This photograph shows a model of the *Britannia* floating in the indoor swimming pool of the *Queen Elizabeth*, the largest passenger ship ever built.

The first four Cunarders all had Latin geographical names ending in –ia—thus starting the famous tradition followed, with very rare exceptions, in the company's history. The first four Cunarders were the *Britannia* (Britain), *Acadia* (Nova Scotia), *Caledonia* (Scotland) and *Columbia* (America). They only carried "cabin" passengers; the poorer voyagers who were emigrating from their homelands to America continued to go on sailing packets, which frequently took from two to three months to make the voyage. In 1840 the cabin shown opposite, top, was luxurious. In 1842 it was occupied by famed British novelist Charles Dickens on his trip to America. His description of how cramped it was, how he hated the passage and how he feared for his life when he saw the live sparks from the funnel shooting up toward the sails might have come right out of one of his novels, it was so rugged and horrific. He returned by sailing packet.

But Cunard did its best to suggest luxury in the tiny "ladies' cabin" amidships on the first four ships. A picture of this room is one of several scenes aboard featured in the "Boston Mails" china. Handsome chandeliers, carved wooden paneling and tufted sofas gave a sense of luxury otherwise missing. The dining saloon could hold two long tables. Passengers sat on long benches on the outer sides of these

tables or on couches alongside the wall. There must have been several sittings for each meal. The first Cunarders had space for 640 tons of coal and 225 tons of cargo. Each burned 38 tons of coal a day. At this point in steamer evolution the engines could be operated steadily, for the condenser had been invented and ships no longer had to use salt water in their boilers. The paddle wheels turned at 16 revolutions per minute and the paddle-wheel boxes were beautifully decorated art objects. The public was well aware that, with these early Cunarders, a new era of oceanic intercourse had begun. [Built by Robert Duncan & Company, Port Glasgow, Scotland, 1840. 1,139 gross tons; 207 feet long; 34 feet wide. Paddle wheels with side lever engines. Service speed 9 knots. 115 cabin passengers.]

HIBERNIA (opposite, bottom).

Cannon salutes, elaborate dinners, toasts and speech-making at both Halifax and Boston marked the arrival of the first Cunarder and the excitement created by the establishment of this important new service. Samuel Cunard had deliberately overestimated the time of the passage so that the public would cheer when the run was made in fewer days. The return voyage, including a stop at Halifax, took just a bit over ten days. This was hailed by the London *Times* as the "quickest communication between the two countries ever effected." Rival steamship lines were established between New York and Bremen and New York and Le Havre. New competing services also ran out of Britain. On her best day, the *Britannia* steamed 280 miles. In mid-Atlantic she passed her sister, the *Acadia*, heading westward. Boston was proud of these early Cunarders as demonstrated in February 1844, when the harbor froze over and a seven-mile channel was cut by citizens of Boston to permit the *Britannia* or one of her sisters to sail. To celebrate this event, a contemporary lithograph was run off and sold in thousands. Then the merchants of Boston, suddenly realizing that the engraving publicized a drawback of their harbor, did their best to buy up all the copies and destroy them. Few survived, but the damage was done: Cunard began to think about moving its western terminus to New York. The first New York visit by a Cunarder was made in 1847 by the *Hibernia*, the first of Cunard's second generation of steamships. Samuel Cunard was prompted to make the move because of word that the United States Congress was considering a subsidy for a new American steamship line from New York—probably the famous Collins Line, which was begun in 1850 with four outstanding new flyers. This woodcut shows the *Hibernia* docked at Jersey City, stern in. [Built by Robert Steele & Company, Greenock, Scotland, 1843. 1,422 gross tons; 219 feet long; 35 feet wide. Paddle wheels with side lever engines. Service speed 9.5 knots. Passenger capacity estimated to have been about 125.]

EUROPA and AMERICA (above).

This fine old print showing two new Cunarders, the *Europa* (in the foreground heading to the left) and the *America* (far right) reveals how slowly sail died on the Atlantic. The look of the steamship is evolving. In due course, both would lose the little mizzen far aft, already looking like a vestigial remnant. Boiler pressure was up to over 18 pounds per square inch, passenger capacity was up to 140 compared to the 115 on the *Britannia*, and size was beginning to cube as both length and beam were increased. But the similarities to sail were also still evident. These ships were still steered from the stern, a method as old as the Phoenicians. Fresh vegetables were kept, as tradition had long dictated, in overturned lifeboats stored atop cabins for the baker and the butcher inboard of the starboard paddle box. The steward's room, in a narrow passage running athwartships, had a window for dispensing spirits. Far forward was a covered capstan, which William Chambers, an English publisher who crossed on the *America* in 1853, described as his favorite spot for smoking and story-telling. But such comments only highlighted the striking differences between Cunard's earlier steamers and those put into service in 1852 by the brash American Edward Knight Collins. His first four beauties were the *Baltic*, *Atlantic*, *Arctic* and *Pacific*. Not only did they break the speed record, but they introduced unheard-of luxuries, such as the annunciator system—a way of providing a bell in each cabin by which the steward could be summoned. Another much-talked-about luxury, particularly appreciated by tobacco-chewing Americans of that time, were the sea-green, shell-encrusted spittoons. Collins in no time stole the cream of the trade from Cunard. But the Collins Line was built on sand. [*Europa:* built by John Wood, Port Glasgow, Scotland, 1848. 1,834 gross tons; 251 feet long; 38 feet wide. Paddle wheels with side lever engines. Service speed 10 knots. 140 cabin passengers. *America:* built by Steele's of Greenock, Greenock, Scotland, 1848. 1,825 gross tons; 251 feet long; 38 feet wide. Paddle wheels with side lever engines. Service speed 10.5 knots. 140 cabin passengers.]

PERSIA (opposite, top).

Naval architects and ship-line executives are slow to change anything. Here, in Cunard's famous *Persia*, built in 1856, we see an example of ultraconservative attitudes and real progress. The ship still has sails and three masts (although earlier Cunarders had had their mizzen-masts removed) and boasts the old clipper bows. American coastal liners had long before adopted the straight stem, and a number of American transatlantic liners had also turned to this style. But not Cunard. On the other hand, this was an iron ship. In 1843 Brunel's famous *Great Britain* had proved that large iron ships would float, but to get Cunard's hidebound naval architects to accept iron was a major development. The two smokestacks were also a departure. The *Persia* was a record-breaker in many ways, and one of the most beautiful of all early Cunarders. She was three times the size of the *Britannia*, built only 16 years earlier. The *Persia* could make 13.5 knots and won the transatlantic speed record immediately. She instituted the custom of

carrying passengers in two classes. The *Persia* was Samuel Cunard's answer to the Collins Line. Her near-sister ship was Cunard's handsome *Scotia* of 1862, the company's last paddle wheeler. Noted British author Henry Fry said of the *Scotia* that she was "the finest, fastest and strongest ship of her day." A more modern authority, Philip Spratt, has called her the last and finest Cunard paddler. She served a remarkable 13 years under Cunard's golden lion house flag. Perhaps most important of all, the *Scotia* helped Cunard designers decide to abandon paddle wheels. Coming out in the same year as the screw steamer *China*, she was a perfect yardstick—all the comparisons favored the propeller-driven vessel! [*Persia:* built by Robert Napiers & Sons Limited, Glasgow, Scotland, 1856. 3,414 gross tons; 360 feet long; 45 feet wide. Paddle wheels with side lever engines. Service speed 13.5 knots. 250 passengers (200 cabin class, 50 second class).]

RUSSIA (opposite, bottom).

Cunard's *Russia* of 1867 retained the clipper bow but abandoned paddle wheels for screw propulsion. Almost 20 years before she was built there had been a dramatic contest between a paddle steamer and a ship moved by a screw propeller. The two vessels had been chained together stern to stern, and the power of the propeller had triumphed by pulling the paddle steamer. But it took another generation to convince many shipowners, and Cunard was no exception. Its success had been based on conservatism and tried-and-true techniques and it was not ready to take the lead in anything but fine service and safe operation. The *Russia* had sails and used them, as did most steamships of the nineteenth century. In fact, the huge German *Vaterland*, built in 1914 and by far the largest steamship built up to that day, had specifications in which it was spelled out that her masts were *not* to be rigged for sail.

Sail died hard on the oceans of the world. Propeller-driven steamers of this period still had good reason to keep sails: If the propeller shaft should break (as did happen in several instances), a ship was able to come in entirely under sail power (albeit two or three weeks late). Of course its owners would be frantic and relatives of passengers aboard would suffer much pain and worry. But until twin screws were adopted sail was still foremost on steamships of the late nineteenth century. The *Russia* was a powerful-looking vessel. She could make 14 knots and won the Blue Ribbon of the Atlantic by steaming from New York to Queenstown in eight days and 25 minutes. For some reason her builders only provided accommodations for 235 in first class. This was later increased to 430 with no apparent difficulty. Copies of this painting, which shows the *Russia* entering Liverpool, were distributed by the Cunard Line for many decades. When the *Russia* was 13 years old, she was sold to the Red Star Line and renamed *Waesland*. She was lost in 1902 in a collision with the *Harmonides*. [Built by J. & G. Thomson Limited, Glasgow, Scotland, 1867. 2,959 gross tons; 358 feet long; 42 feet wide. Inverted engines, single screw. Service speed 14 knots. 235 first-class passengers.]

The Persia was built by the Lairds Brothers of Birkenhead, England, for the Cunard Steamship Company in 1855. Length 360 feet, breadth 45 ft., depth 35' and was the largest ship of her class then afloat. She was the turning-point of a new movement in ship-building, being the first ocean steamship built of Steel. Her maiden voyage was from Liverpool to Halifax Nova Scotia, thence to Boston Mass.

SERVIA (above).

Some have called the *Servia* of 1881 the first superliner, although the term itself did not originate until 1929. She was, nonetheless, a remarkable advance in naval architecture. Coming just 41 years after the *Britannia*, the *Servia* made 17.8 knots on her trials. Her main dining saloon, 74 feet long and 49 feet wide, could seat 350 passengers. She was a single-screw, two-stacked beauty with three masts and a full set of square sails, fore and aft sails and headsails. Her stacks were widely spaced. Most significant, perhaps, she was the first Cunarder to be built of steel and the first Cunarder to be lighted with electricity. There is no question that the *Servia* was the first of a new generation of Cunarders. Even with sails she looked like a steamer. She had a straight stem and a graceful rounded or counter stern. She had what was quite new for that day, a "turtle-back" sterncastle, rounded and unobstructed so water could roll off it with ease. Her passenger spaces were much more elegant than those of her earlier sisters under the Cunard house flag. There were 202 cabins for first-class passengers. Her officers and crew totaled 200. Special features included suites with double beds, dressing areas and wardrobes. The *Servia* began her maiden voyage from Liverpool to New York on November 26, 1881. So rapid was the evolution of the ocean liner, however, that this superb ship served only 20 years. At the end of her hundred seventy-first round-trip she was retired, sold to the Thomas W. Ward scrap yard and towed to Preston for dismantling. [Built by J. & G. Thomson Limited, Glasgow, 1881. 7,391 gross tons; 532 feet long; 52 feet wide. Compound engines, single screw. Service speed 17 knots. 1,050 passengers (450 first class, 600 third class).]

AURANIA (opposite, top).

Now the hull boasted two long rows of portholes, not just one. The bow even had three, being a deck higher to offer greater hull strength against oncoming waves. There were still three masts (with top masts); still two funnels. The turtle-back arrangement looked modern. The two aftermost lifeboats are both swung out, ready to be lowered immediately if needed. This illustrates nicely how the shepherd's hook–style davits worked. It also shows to excellent advantage the beautifully styled lapstraked lifeboats themselves. The ratlines were still needed by seamen to climb up the masts. As ships became larger, the masts were increased in diameter and were soon

large enough to contain steel ladders for safer ascent. A really close look will show that the stern deck (poop or sterncastle) is jammed with soldiers. The ship is under tow, and may be taking soldiers to the Boxer Rebellion. [Built by J. & G. Thomson Limited, Clydebank, Scotland, 1883. 7,269 gross tons; 485 feet long; 57 feet wide. Compound engines, single screw. Service speed 17.5 knots. 1,180 passengers (480 cabin class, 700 third class).]

ETRURIA (opposite, bottom).

With this new liner, built in 1884, and her maiden-voyage departure on April 25, 1886, Cunard began a gradual change to what is today accepted as good ship dimensions—wider hull, proportionately shorter ships. The combination of old styling with new thinking continued, however. The *Etruria* had three masts and was fitted for sails. Although she was somewhat shorter than the greyhound *Servia*, she was larger, had greater horsepower and could go faster. She was the last single-screw ship to break the Atlantic speed record. Among the most exciting features of her design were her two wonderful funnels. Twice as thick as those on the *Servia*, they seemed huge. Naval architects were beginning to realize that a ship's smokestacks were her chief point of identification. A three-stacked liner had already been built, others were under construction. Four-stacked ships were on the drawing boards. Slowly, what was to be the pattern of travel classes was being created. *Etruria* began as a two-class ship and was rebuilt to have three classes, adding a second class of 160. No one apparently minded these distinctions. The poorer classes were those who were emigrating, and their very decision to pull up roots and change their way of life spelled optimism for the future. Whereas early Cunard ships had been entirely for the well-off, Cunard management of the *Etruria*'s era had come to realize that the money was really in large third-class lists. First class brought the prestige, but third the income. France, which had quickly joined the ranks of Atlantic liner operators, Germany and Italy, realized this even more than did the British. New immigrant-carriers were sliding off the ways in all these nations at an increasing rate. [Built by John Elder & Company, Glasgow, Scotland, 1884. 8,127 gross tons; 520 feet long; 57 feet wide. Compound engines, single screw. Service speed 19 knots. 1,350 passengers (550 cabin class, 800 third class).]

CAMPANIA (opposite, top).

Here, at last, is a real steamship, with real smokestacks, raked to perfection, thick enough and just the right height to dominate the ship. They measured 19 feet in diameter. From keel to top they rose 130 feet. What a superb counter stern, elegant and perfectly designed, and what a sharp, knifelike bow (that, for the next several generations, would be the ideal)! The *Campania* and her sister ship the *Lucania* put Cunard on top from the design standpoint and just about every other as the century came to a close. Her particulars were awe-inspiring. She had 13 boilers with 100 furnaces and consumed 20.5 tons of coal per hour. Her 30,000 indicated horsepower could produce a top speed of 22 knots. Her tonnage was 12,950—still way below that of the *Great Eastern* (built before the Civil War and not to be exceeded in tonnage until early in the twentieth century). Although the *Campania* was launched September 8, 1892, she did not make her maiden voyage until April 22 of the next year, when she set a new transatlantic record on her eastbound crossing: five days, 17 hours and 27 minutes. Her twin screws (Cunard's first) had been pioneered by the French and by Inman Line steamers. Sails could finally be abandoned (although they may have been carried aboard) and the ship's superstructure could rise tier upon tier, deck upon deck, as can be seen here in the five-deck-high forward bridge. The helmsman had to be forward and he had to be high to see over the bow. [Built by Fairfield Shipbuilding & Engineering Company, Govan, Scotland, 1893. 12,950 gross tons; 622 feet long; 65 feet wide. Steam triple expansion engines, twin screw. Service speed 22 knots. 2,000 passengers (600 first class, 400 second class, 1,000 third class).]

LUCANIA (opposite, bottom).

There was a definite plan in Cunard smokestack design in the days before the *Queen Elizabeth 2*. The divisions of the stacks were even, as can be seen perfectly here, in a view of the *Lucania* at anchor at Liverpool. The small enclosed wheelhouse, five decks above the main deck, and the beginnings of a well-designed forward superstructure face can also be seen here. The main deck is flush from the stem to the stern, open amidships but with no well deck forward dividing the forecastle or poop from the rest of the ship. (The *Queen Mary* took a step backward in this particular feature.) The bridge really looks like a bridge. Open stairs lead up from the roof of the cabins on the boat

deck. The picture also shows the huge air funnels, which were painted white outside and red inside. Sixteen can be counted here, all facing forward to get the wind. Before forced draft, they were vital to make the bowels of this ship inhabitable for the crews of strong-armed firemen shoveling coal at a almost death-defying rate. It was not unusual for a new man to drop unconscious from the effort. There was no shortage of lifeboats at this point: plenty for all passengers and crew. [Built by Fairfield Shipbuilding & Engineering Company, Govan, Scotland, 1893. 12,950 gross tons; 620 feet long; 65 feet wide. Steam triple expansion engines, twin screw. Service speed 22 knots. 2,000 passengers (600 first class, 400 second class, 1,000 third class).]

SINKING OF THE CAMPANIA, 1918 (above).

Both the lovely *Lucania* and the classic *Campania* met sad endings. Neither sailed very long. The *Lucania*, not quite 16 years old, was gutted by a fire at her pier at Liverpool. Her engines were not damaged and she was able to steam to the ship breakers' yard at Swansea, where she was scrapped in 1910. The *Campania* suffered an even greater disaster while in the hands of the British Navy. She had been sold to scrappers in 1914, but was saved when the Navy bought her and converted her into an aircraft carrier. Her forward stack was replaced with two thin smoke pipes placed athwartships, and great booms were built to serve a short flight deck aft. The *Campania's* short naval life was brought to an abrupt end when the battleship *Revenge* collided with her on November 5, 1918 in the Firth of Forth. She sank by the stern, with two battleships standing by. This was a critical period for Cunard. As the new century dawned, the American financier J. P. Morgan tried to win a monopoly on Atlantic shipping, buying the famous White Star Line and several other major companies and making agreements with large German, Dutch and Belgian ship lines. The British government was so concerned by his successes that it offered Cunard a very large building and operation subsidy if the line would remain independent and build the two largest and fastest ships in the world. As a result, the *Lusitania* and *Mauretania* were constructed for Cunard and entered service only a decade after the entry of the *Campania* and *Lucania*. This new pair was almost three times as large and represented tremendous advances in power, speed and accommodations.

SAXONIA.

The *Saxonia*'s stack is believed to have been the tallest ever put on a liner—106 feet from deck level to cowl top, although her nearly identical sister ship, the *Ivernia*, had a funnel of similar size. The *Saxonia* was England's answer to such ships as the *Graf Waldersee*, built in 1898 by the Hamburg-America Line and able to carry 162 in first class, 184 in second and 2,200 in third. She had three sisters, all with equally large passenger capacity. The *Saxonia* was also one of the earliest Cunarders (if not the very first) built by John Brown of Clydebank, Glasgow, the builders of Cunard's two greatest Queens. Definitely not a flyer, she was a new type of liner for Cunard. Her maiden voyage began on May 22, 1900 at Liverpool and she went to Boston—not New York. Her four masts were installed for a very practical purpose: She had considerable cargo space and the booms were needed. Above all, she was a money-maker, as was the *Ivernia* and her near-sister ship, the famous *Carpathia*. She was built when Cunard was battling bravely to keep out of the clutches of Morgan's International Mercantile Marine. In this view, the *Saxonia* is riding high out of the water and swinging on her starboard bow anchor chain. The tall stack has the same even divisions that mark it as Cunard's.

The women's hats visible in the deck scene shown opposite suggest the date was a mid-June sailing day in 1924. Lifeboats are swung out over the side, evidence that it had to be a summer sailing, with little danger of severe rolling. The boat deck is packed with passengers staking out their claims to deck chairs in a most determined fashion. This *Herald Tribune* view, taken by a staff photographer named Steffen, has a caption noting that the ship carried 460 college students—"armed with ukeleles, saxophones, banjos and cameras—and what a jolly party it was." These solid citizens, however, far from being college students, must have been passengers in first class, as their boat-deck space indicates. After the moment of sailing, the boats may have been brought inboard, cutting the deck space down by two-thirds. The *Saxonia* had been transferred to the Mediterranean run in 1911, operating between Trieste and New York until the First World War. After that "war to end all wars," she was placed on the Liverpool–to–New York run until she was sold to ship breakers in Holland in March 1926. The *Ivernia* did not survive the war: She was sunk on January 1, 1917, off Cape Matapán, with the loss of 36 lives. The third ship in the trio was the *Carpathia*, which was slightly smaller and came out in 1903. Her name lives on as the ship that rescued the few passengers who survived the sinking of the famous White Star liner *Titanic*. [Built by John Brown & Company Limited, Clydebank, Scotland, 1900. 14,197 gross tons; 600 feet long; 64 feet wide. Steam quadruple expansion engines, twin screw. Service speed 16 knots. 1,960 passengers (160 first class, 200 second class, 1,600 third class).]

Some Early Cunarders

CARPATHIA (above).

The *Carpathia* was laid down in 1902 and began her maiden crossing on May 5, 1903. She was on the Liverpool-to-Boston service with her slightly larger sisters the *Saxonia* and the *Ivernia*. A voyage took nine days. Her stack was not quite as tall as that on her two sisters. She had the four masts then the rule for large passenger–cargo carriers. She also had a pronounced sheer from bow to stern. Her white boot-topping above the waterline, always a distinctive Cunard adornment, gave her added class. Her fame has continued, even expanded, over the years, because of her role in the *Titanic* rescue on April 15, 1912. An entire issue of the *Titanic Commutator*, a magazine published by the Titanic Historical Society, was devoted to this sturdy vessel. Artifacts from her, such as menus, deck plans, passenger lists and concert programs, are today priced almost as high as memorabilia from the *Titanic* herself. This heroic ship was sunk by a German submarine on July 17, 1918, near Bishop Rock. Three torpedoes hit her and five men in her boiler room were killed in the ensuing explosions. [Built by Swan & Hunter Limited, Newcastle, England, 1903. 13,603 gross tons; 558 feet long; 64 feet wide. Steam quadruple expansion engines, twin screw. Service speed 14 knots. 1,704 passengers (204 first class, 1,500 third class).]

CARONIA (1905; opposite, top).

Another striking liner of the new style emerged from the drawing boards of Cunard draftsmen in 1904–05—the beautiful *Caronia*. Here was the culmination of the design changes begun with the *Aurania*, when Cunarders became wider and higher than the earlier grey-hounds. The *Caronia* was another steamer built by John Brown. She had a gross tonnage of nearly 20,000—the biggest Cunarder yet. Her maiden voyage from Liverpool began on February 25, 1905. Of course, she was on the New York run, the world's premier ocean-liner route. She was important for another reason: The turbine engine had been invented and Cunard wanted to test it by putting it in one of two otherwise identical ships to see whether it would be wise to install turbines in the new "monster" twins, the *Lusitania* and the *Mauretania*. The company was building two forerunners of the *Caronia* class. So in the second, the *Carmania*, turbine propulsion was installed. The *Caronia* had the standard quadruple expansion recipro-cating engines which, with twin screws, gave her an 18-knot speed. Also built by John Brown, so that everything else in the test would be

equal, the *Carmania* proved to be the faster by over two knots, making 20.4 during her trials.

The smokestacks on the *Caronia* and the *Carmania* were not as tall in proportion to the height of the ship's superstructure as had been the case with earlier Cunarders of the turn of the century. Therefore, the divisions were only four, not five, the black part being one quarter of the ship's stack while the two thin black bands separated the orange-red section into three equal portions. This held on Cunarders through the new *Caronia* of 1948 and the 1954–57 quartet *Carinthia*, *Ivernia*, *Saxonia* and *Sylvania*.

Both ships had long and profitable careers of 27 years. Well liked by transatlantic and cruise passengers, they were affectionately dubbed "the pretty sisters." Both served in the First World War, the *Carmania* in a spectacular fashion. She was converted into an armed auxiliary cruiser and, on September 14, 1914, met and then sank the German liner *Cap Trafalgar*, which was also serving the same way, although no means as well converted. The *Carmania* survived despite having received 79 hits. Both Cunard ships resumed regular Atlantic service, operating until sold for scrap in 1932. The *Caronia* sailed to Japan under the name of *Taiseiyo Maru* for demolition; the *Carmania* was scrapped in Britain. [Built by John Brown & Company Limited, Clydebank, Scotland, 1905. 19,524 gross tons; 678 feet long; 72 feet wide. Steam quadruple expansion engines, twin screw. Service speed 18 knots. 2,650 passengers (300 first class, 350 second class, 900 third class, 1,100 steerage).]

CARMANIA (1905; opposite, bottom).

The interiors of the *Caronia* and *Carmania* were traditional, as the *Carmania*'s elegant first-class dining saloon shows. Long tables, potted palms, fixed swivel chairs, fluted columns and pilasters with gilt trim were the rule. The saloon was well down in the hull of the ship, light coming through curtained sideports. The *Caronia* and her sister ship had such modern outlines that the evolution of great liners seemed to come to a halt. Through the prewar period and even into much of the twenties and thirties, basic lines went largely unchanged. For nearly 40 years, their classic bridge face continued to be the standard. Streamlining did not enter Cunard's picture until just before the Second World War. There were, however, great changes in liner styling, made for esthetic reasons and because of the abrupt ending of mass immigration after the First World War.

THE BIG THREE: "THE FAST SHIPS"

CUNARD BUILT THREE SUPERLINERS before the First World War, but lost one, the *Lusitania*, in 1915. After the war Cunard acquired another superliner from Germany, the *Imperator*, which was renamed the *Berengaria*. The *Mauretania, Aquitania* and *Berengaria* were the Cunard's postwar Big Three.

The *Lusitania* and the *Mauretania* had been, in a sense, the gift of the British government to Cunard to insure that Cunard remained an independent British company in the face of the creation of Morgan's vast international shipping cartel, the International Mercantile Marine. His was an ambitious scheme that might have succeeded. The world is probably fortunate, however, that it did not, because competition has always been the spice of transatlantic shipping.

As a result of the encouragement offered by the British government came two of the finest ships ever built. Some say that, from many standpoints, the *Mauretania* was the most beautiful, most successful and perhaps the greatest passenger liner ever built. Certainly she was the favorite of countless thousands. She held the transatlantic speed record longer than any other ship. She did heroic service as a troopship in the First World War, and, painted white, she was used extensively and successfully as a cruise ship near the end of her life. There can be little doubt that the *Lusitania* would have done as well had she not been sunk by a German submarine in the war—a sinking that influenced history as few other ship disasters have. From the standpoint of beauty of outline, it is hard to name any competitors for the styling and handsomeness of the *Lusitania* and the *Mauretania*. From any angle they were just about perfect. The decision by Cunard to have the four stacks equally spaced, rather than in pairs, was brilliant. It gave a unity to their design that made the German four-stackers look old-fashioned. The added height of the stacks on the *Mauretania* and the *Lusitania* was another main point in their favor in contrast to the German four-stack pioneers. Above all, the decision to have only a fore- and a mainmast was crucial in creating the integrity of design that gave such success to the basic outline, especially when seen from far off. They were the classic beauties that old sailors of today look back upon with nostalgia.

Although there are many who would probably dispute us, our feelings about the *Aquitania* and the *Berengaria* are not entirely so enthusiastic. Each had its grand points, and each has its defenders—but neither came up to the dazzling perfection of the *Mauretania* and *Lusitania*, in our opinion. There are those for whom the *Aquitania* was the greatest. Her career saw her survive both wars to steam on as the last of the four-stackers. By the same token, the *Berengaria* wrote history from her very beginning as the world's first ship to exceed 50,000 gross tons. When Cunard took her after the war as a reparation to replace the *Lusitania*, she served for a time as the R.M.S. *Imperator*. Cunard made her the "in" ship of the 1920s. Even the dogs who sailed aboard her were the "rich and famous" dogs, like Rin-Tin-Tin.

LUSITANIA.

"Limitation of language makes adequate word description of these mammoth Cunarders impossible," a 1908 brochure of photographs of the *Lusitania* and *Mauretania* said. "The Cunard Line, unrivalled for the safety with which it has carried its thousands upon thousands of passengers, now offers to its patrons the *Lusitania* and *Mauretania*, the safest, fastest, most magnificent steamships in the world."

As lifeboats are being tested at the ship's New York pier in 1907 or 1908, hundreds stand around admiring the lines of the world's largest ship, the *Lusitania*, and the Cunard golden lion house flag waves proudly in the breeze at the truck of the mainmast. The new-style patent anchor is recessed in an oval hull indentation. Scratches on the shiny black paint on the hull had been made on the way to Quarantine. The modified "lighthouse" for the green starboard running light is just under the wing of the bridge. In earlier ships it stood alone farther forward, an actual little lighthouse on many new liners, one on either side for the green and red lights. Cunard was one of the first lines on the Atlantic, if not the first, to adopt the custom of having green for port and red for starboard. In earlier days, ships had sailed with no lights, relying on a signaling cannon to warn other ships in fog. [Built by John Brown & Company Limited, Clydebank, Scotland, 1907. 31,550 gross tons; 787 feet long; 87 feet wide. Steam turbines, quadruple screw. Service speed 25 knots. 2,165 passengers (563 first class, 464 second class, 1,138 third class).]

MAURETANIA.

Two major points of difference between the *Mauretania* and the *Lusitania* can be seen by comparing this photograph with that preceding. The *Mauretania*'s A-deck promenade, beginning after the third lifeboat, has been extended out over the hull. This promenade, therefore, has a slight overhang above the promenade on B deck. The huge air funnels on either side of the pilot house are much more evident than the lower and less-obvious air funnels on the *Lusitania*. This superb bow view of the 1920s, the flags all standing out bravely in the breeze, shows the heroically proportioned new flyer at anchor off Quarantine on Staten Island in New York Harbor. The white boot-topping has been washed off in the rough westbound crossing just finished. Five outlets pour streams of water from the engine areas into New York harbor. An old steam tug is overwhelmed by the size of the liner. A seaman halfway up the foremast, probably the new watch-lookout, holds on to the tarred ratlines as he climbs to the commodious crow's nest. The thin, perfectly perpendicular stem of this ship and her ill-fated sister were often described as "knifelike." The same configuration extended down to the rounded forefoot and keel. No one realized at that time that this knifelike penetration of the water created a massive vacuum pocket at either side and cost thousands of dollars in added fuel each trip.

An unusual feature, and one frequently dispensed with in smaller liners, was the docking bridge *(above)*. With the *Mauretania*, it was essential because of the ship's tremendous length, greater than that of many modern cruise liners whose tonnage may be a third more or even double the *Mauretania*'s. This great length-to-beam ratio was partly responsible for her extraordinary speed. It also made for a decidedly less comfortable ride and, for many, a high incidence of mal de mer. This was the price of being the "world's fastest liner" and Blue Ribbon speed queen for longer than any other ship ever built. The beautiful counter stern is a chief feature of this lovely view, taken in 1931. The ship is about to move carefully out from her slip north of Pier 54 at West 14 Street, Manhattan. She was drawing a bit less than 35 feet aft at this point, much deeper than many of today's huge cruise ships, with drafts often of 22 feet or less. The port of New York had a tough time keeping a 35-foot channel dredged for great liners of the twenties and thirties. The *Leviathan* drew 41 feet, believed to be the deepest draft of any great liner. The canvas shield in the middle of the aft docking bridge was to protect the helmsman from the wind should the emergency steering wheel there have to be used. [Built by Swan, Hunter & Wigham Richardson Limited, Newcastle, England, 1907. 31,938 gross tons; 790 feet long; 88 feet wide. Steam turbines, quadruple screw. Service speed 25 knots. 2,335 passengers (560 first class, 475 second class, 1,300 third class).]

The *Mauretania*. The *Mauretania* was a member of that very select group known as the "floating palaces." Her interiors represented the very best design and decoration from Britain, and that of Europe as well. The woods that were used, for example, were selected from British and French forests. The carving was done with exacting detail. Decoration ranged from French Renaissance to English Country. Certainly, the liner's first-class main lounge *(opposite, top; above)*, capped by a large domed skylight and featuring a marble fireplace at the far end, was among her finest rooms.

Public rooms such as this were quite modern for the time—much less ornate than the period's French or German liners, with all their carved cherubs, armored knights, large-bosomed goddesses and bacchanalian figures. Although they were completely out of place and impractical, fireplaces were considered a high point in elegance on ships. They were usually entirely artificial, having electrically lighted logs, but people loved to sit around them. Great domed skylights were usually in the center of the ship, where they would be protected from the pounding of huge seas. (The early Inman Line queens *City of Paris* and *City of New York* had them forward of the bridge, where they were continually subjected to wave damage.) During the *Mauretania*'s trooping days in the First World War, paneling and marble pilasters such as these were all carefully protected with coverings of wood and cloth. When the ship was scrapped at Jarrow, Scotland, and

the paneling removed to be sold at auction, it was found that during the ship's various refits certain shaftlike areas between rooms, extending down many decks, had been filled with shavings, old rags and odd scraps—all highly inflammable. The fact that the *Mauretania* never had any fatal fires is a tribute to excellent maintenance and her fire watch.

The *Mauretania*'s first-class dining saloon *(opposite, bottom)* was a two-deck affair, with tables on both levels. Some of the writing in contemporary brochures makes interesting reading:

> When the ship is in evening dress, this dining room is as gay and brilliant as the Armenonville in Paris' famous Bois, as socially correct as the Berkeley in London, as impressive for its notables as the Ambassador or the Ritz in New York. It offers a menu which is as cosmopolitan as the people who chatter around the tables.

This view shows the captain's table in the center, with a monster arrangement of palms and long-stemmed greens rising up into the balcony area. Later, the center portion under the dome was kept free of tables and used for dancing during the dinner hour. "Dining in the *Mauretania*," a later brochure noted, "thus becomes, more than ever, a sparkling affair." For some reason the first-class dining saloon on the *Lusitania* did not seem to have such spaciousness or excitement.

The Mauretania. On a great liner the verandah cafe (always spelled with the "h") added prestige and éclat. When new, this space on the *Mauretania (above)* was open to the stern, as on German liners of the day, with much heavier furniture and smaller windows at either side. This picture, from a sepia-toned postcard printed after the First World War, shows how Cunard made the space more usable in all kinds of weather by adding a glass wall aft and much larger windows port and starboard. Wicker chairs and tables and a new linoleum floor were installed. Rounded columns were substituted for austere square, fluted columns. The original room was more dignified and had no hanging flowers or potted plants. In the newer configuration, the glass skylight had many more panes and was higher.

In dazzle-paint camouflage *(opposite, top)* is the beautiful *Mauretania* during the First World War—a monument to man's stupidity—in which the *Lusitania* was lost on May 7, 1915, sunk in minutes with 1,198 lives sacrificed to the tortured aims of the politicians, admirals and generals on both sides. Most recent scholarship has offered the well-supported theory that the British deliberately provoked the sinking by a German submarine, hoping that the hue and cry would bring America into the war on Britain's side. And, in due course, it did, although initially there were millions of pro-German Americans who would have sided with the Kaiser.

The *Mauretania* had two close calls during her restoration for peacetime service. She was being rebuilt in a British shipyard when a strike halted all work and threatened to delay her completion. It was finally decided to take her under tow, without her own engine power, to a French yard. While she was crossing the Channel to France, a bad storm swooped down and the tugs lost their tow. Powerless and with only a small crew aboard, the *Mauretania* found herself in gale conditions, unable to steer or save herself in any way. Fortunately, the brave tug men eventually regained control and the tow was completed. The chief engineer in charge watched every step of the work below decks in the French yard and, when things were ready, ordered a dockside test of the 68,000-horsepower engines. He listened over his beloved Parsons turbines like a doctor with a stethoscope. Suddenly he stopped and halted all further testing. Something was wrong. He ordered the turbine involved taken apart, piece by piece. Inside, at the very center, he found a collar button. Had the turbine been turned over, the engine would have been destroyed. French shipyard workers were deliberately sabotaging the work to keep the ship in the yard longer. The engine was saved because of the keenness of the Cunard chief engineer. The ship was restored and appeared as seen here in a 1931 view taken in New York *(opposite, bottom)*, flags flying and ready to do the job she was built for—to serve the traveling public in peacetime.

AQUITANIA.

Cunard's weekly express service, with a sailing in each direction every week from Liverpool (and later Southampton) and from New York, required a trio of large, fast liners. The company already had its successful pair, the *Mauretania* and the *Lusitania*, but, by 1910, needed a third "fast ship," as these superliners were sometimes called. Of course, its rivals had plans of their own. White Star was already building the *Olympic* and then the *Titanic*, and had plans for a third, originally to be called the *Gigantic*, but christened the *Britannic*. But it was the Hamburg-America Line that was building the largest of all, three successively larger liners, the *Imperator*, the *Vaterland* and, finally, the *Bismarck*. Cunard had to keep pace to retain its position in the increasingly competitive North Atlantic trade. For their third superliner, the Liverpool directors and designers opted for a vessel larger than the *Mauretania* or the *Lusitania* (in fact, some 15,000 tons greater and about 100 feet longer), but decided against extremely powerful machinery, eliminating any attempt at winning the Blue Ribbon. The trophy would be left to the *Mauretania*. The new ship would copy the four-funnel design, but certainly to better effect, and otherwise would differ only in that her interiors would be somewhat more splendid.

The *Lusitania*'s builders, John Brown & Company on the Clyde, were selected to build the new ship, which was named the *Aquitania* (after the Roman province in southwest France), on April 21, 1913. The Brown yards would become a favorite with Cunard, later creating the *Queen Mary*, the *Queen Elizabeth*, the *Caronia* and the *Queen Elizabeth 2*. Unfortunately, the *Aquitania* had barely entered service, beginning in May 1914, when the First World War erupted. After a few trips to New York, she was called to military duty, first as an armed merchant cruiser, then as a troopship and still later as a hospital ship. While major passenger ships, such as the *Aquitania*, the

Mauretania and the *Lusitania*, had been intended from the start to be used as armed merchant cruisers in the event of war, it was soon discovered that these ships were far too vulnerable to the menace of German U-boats. Instead, they were better suited as troopers.

The *Aquitania* was almost immediately dubbed the "Ship Beautiful." This cachet, which lasted throughout her career (1914–49), applied not only to her serenely, almost perfectly balanced exterior, but to her splendid interiors as well. Surely, the columned Palladian lounge *(opposite, top)*, which rose two decks, was one of the finest rooms ever to put to sea. Another was the Jacobean smoking room *(opposite, bottom)*, which was copied from the Royal Naval College in Greenwich, London. In those high-spirited days prior to the First World War, it was common for the designers and decorators of the big liners to imitate shoreside palaces, the mansions and great country homes. There were also touches of the exotic—Arabian and Egyptian, Persian and Moorish.

A close study of the A-deck deck plan on the *Aquitania* shows that the two-deck-high Jacobean smoking room aft was really six rooms in one. Its central portion—forward—was what most voyagers remembered as *the* smoking room, but to the left and right of its forward end were two smaller one-deck-high areas, enclosed on three sides, which had all the atmosphere of separate public rooms. The after portion was divided by walls jutting out from bow and stern so that, again, a feeling of three separate rooms was created. Exquisite fluted pilasters and columns, carved wooden panels, two-deck-high windows on the sides and beamed ceilings all contributed to the "Old English" feeling of this handsome assembly of cordial spaces where passengers could chat, play cards or simply relax. [Built by John Brown & Company Limited, Clydebank, Scotland, 1914. 45,647 gross tons; 901 feet long; 97 feet wide. Steam turbines, twin screw. 3,230 passengers (618 first class, 614 second class, 1,998 third class).]

The Aquitania. After heroic war duties, the *Aquitania* was refurbished to her original luxurious standard. With the work being done at Newcastle (from where the ship is shown departing in 1919; *above*), Cunard sensibly used this refitting period to convert the liner as well. Like almost all of the major liners, her propulsion system was changed from coal to oil fuel. And so, in the years just following the Great War, the age of those 200 or so stokers, the infamous "Black Gangs," was brought to a close. By the summer of 1920, the *Aquitania* was back, more efficient than ever, on the commercial Atlantic trade.

In the 1920s, the *Aquitania* settled down to an extremely successful and highly profitable career. Teamed as part of the "Big Three," along with the *Mauretania* and the *Berengaria* (the largest of the trio), she was noted for her luxurious charm and reliability. In later years, she earned her nickname of "Grand Old Lady." Royalty and aristocracy, politicians and Hollywood film stars were often photographed along her upper decks and in her lavish lounges. In the scene right, the great ship is resting in the Southampton graving dock for a periodic hull cleaning and painting.

Many Cunarders made Saturday morning departures from New York for British and Continental ports: London, Southampton, Liverpool, Cobh (named Queenstown until 1922), Greenock and Belfast, Cherbourg, Le Havre and sometimes to Hamburg. In a scene dating from the summer of 1929 (*left*) families, friends and other visitors are returning ashore 30 minutes prior to the sailing of the *Aquitania*. The *Mauretania* is also shown (*above*) at the same Manhattan piers, across the slip from one of the intermediate liners, the *Samaria*.

CUNARD CREWS.

For many decades, Cunard was one of the most illustrious and best-known shipping companies. Its superb reputation, one of high standards, safety and punctuality, spread well beyond the North Atlantic. To be employed by Cunard was considered prestigious in itself. Often, special contacts were needed for employment. One officer recalled, "It was like working for the Bank of England." The officers in particular were career men, often with over 40 or 50 years of service. The commanders, such as Captain McRostie, seen here on the bridge of the *Mauretania* in the twenties, were a distinctive breed.

AQUITANIA *(below; opposite).*

Before the 1950s, when tugs made the transition to diesel power, steam tugs, their tall, pencil-like funnels often belching smoke, did the job of docking and undocking the liners. These were the "workhorses" of the great ports such as New York, Southampton, London and Liverpool. Often they met the great liners in the early, predawn hours of arrival. For midnight sailings, their work was slightly more complicated, for they had to shift and position the great ships in the pitch black of night. The steam tugs were less maneuverable and less powerful and so, as seen in this view *(below)* of the docking of the *Aquitania* on July 5, 1931, six tugs are at work forward and, out of the view, four more are aft on the starboard side—a total of ten tugs. Today, two tugs can handle the equally large *Queen Elizabeth 2.*

A view *(opposite, top)* looks aft on the *Aquitania*'s starboard upper promenade, deck A, off the end of which the smoking room opens. The photograph was made at sea, July 2, 1931. Even with two rows of big, old-fashioned deck chairs there is plenty of room in which to walk two or three abreast. That was "liner style" luxury.

All of the great liners had the occasional mishap and the Cunarders, even the biggest ones, were no exception. In 1920, during the *Aquitania*'s postwar refit at Newcastle, there was an engine-room explosion. One crew member was killed. In the mid-thirties, she went aground twice—once at Calshot Spit (she was refloated in two-and-a-half hours) and once off Southampton while inbound from a Mediterranean cruise during a 60-mile-an-hour gale that kept her tightly in place for 26 hours before she was freed by 11 tugs. It was during this last incident that this aerial photo *(opposite, bottom)* was taken.

The *Aquitania*. Everett Viez, one of the greatest photographers and photograph collectors of ocean liners, particularly in the years between the two world wars, visited many of the most noted ships and sailed aboard some of them. In a view of July 2, 1931 *(opposite, top)*, he photographed his father, William A. J. Viez, in the bow section of the mighty *Aquitania*. Their voyage together was a short but memorable weekend round-trip cruise between New York and Halifax.

A view of the full foredeck of the *Aquitania (opposite, bottom)*, shows how huge it really was. The preceding photograph was made just below the forward end of the two cargo booms. The two huge air funnels, a distinctive feature, were big enough to be seen in most shots of the *Aquitania*.

Economic conditions on the North Atlantic route were constantly changing. A slump set in in the late twenties, particularly in the number of low-fare passengers in third class. Certainly, the prewar age of mass emigration to the United States was long over, its place being taken by more comfortable tourist class. Consequently, during a major winter overhaul in 1926, the *Aquitania*'s passenger configuration was changed from 618 to 610 in first class, 614 up to 950 in second class and third class, formerly 1,998, reduced to 640 in renamed tourist class.

By the mid-thirties, ships such as the *Aquitania* were already 20 years old and, in some ways, looking out-of-date when compared to the new, sleek, Art Deco generation of Atlantic liners. Consequently, most of the Cunarders were periodically updated and improved to remain competitive. When new suites were added to the *Aquitania*, a Cunard press release read:

> You should see the new suites on the *Aquitania*. They're really quite extraordinary. Quite large and not at all the sort of thing that the seasoned traveller has in mind when he speaks of a ship's stateroom. They're rather like charming guest rooms in delightful homes. In fact a few of the suites have Sun Rooms in which the walls have been treated to resemble stone, carrying out the country house idea, you know. We are remodelling all our fast ships—*Aquitania, Berengaria* and *Mauretania*—making the rooms larger and more beautiful, and adding a number of private baths and showers. It is one of the reasons why the best people are found travelling Cunard!

A photograph of ca. 1926 *(above)* shows the handsome lines of the *Aquitania* as she arrives off New York's Quarantine Station in the Lower Bay for inspection. Several smaller boats—the U.S. Customs, Immigration and Health cutters and the U.S. mail boat, are in attendance.

The Aquitania. In the early thirties, transatlantic traffic slumped so drastically that great liners such as the *Aquitania* often had more crew members than passengers on board. One alternative to lay-up or, far worse, the scrappers, was to send the *Aquitania* on cruises—some luxurious runs, such as New York to the Mediterranean for eight weeks, others less expensive, such as six days from Southampton to Gibraltar and return (and for £5!). Later, she even did some charter service, including a troop voyage out to Palestine for the British government. However, she remained an exceptional and beloved ship. Even in the thirties, when she reached 20, she often had runs of over 24 knots—well above her service speed. Cunard decided, even in

the economically severe Depression years, to invest further in the "Ship Beautiful." She was extensively refitted again, in 1933, a job employing 1,000 workmen for three months. Among the changes and improvements was one special addition: a "sound cinema."

In a magnificent night view the starboard air funnel on foredeck can be clearly seen. The old pilot house has been replaced. The top one was added, as can be clearly seen. The original bridge face ended with the lower pilothouse. But the ship was so huge that her officers could not see well enough over her vast foredeck and the higher vantage point was created. It looked like an afterthought and damaged the beauty of the superstructure's forward design.

The *Aquitania*. A splendid view of the bridge face *(above, top)* from far forward shows the two tall air funnels, and the more pleasing aspect of the bridge before the new upper bridge was added. The second pilot house, it might be noted, was not much more than half the size of the original.

A symphony of red air funnels *(above, bottom)*. No other liner, except the *Mauretania*, ever approached this gaudy elegance. A three-throated brass whistle is high up on the forward smokestack.

The *Aquitania*. A close-up of the forward superstructure *(above)*, taken with the cargo booms forming an interesting pattern overhead, two on either side of the yellow foremast rising from amid the electric cargo-handling engines on a small raised deckhouse. The proud and beautiful *Aquitania* always seemed to suffer because she had no sister ship. She was truly one of a kind and the last of the four-stackers. When she was finally retired, four years after the end of the Second World War, Frank Braynard was a reporter on the New York *Herald Tribune*. He went to the city editor, Joseph Hershberg, and insisted in half a dozen ways that there had to be an editorial about her long life and sad demise. Barely looking up, Hershberg smiled in a tired sort of way and replied, "O.K. you do it." Braynard did, it was used and they paid him all of $7 extra that month.

Twilight of an era: A wintry setting *(below)* frames the last of the Atlantic's grand four-stackers, the *Aquitania*. In the mid-thirties, when the likes of the *Mauretania* and the *Olympic* were sent off to the scrappers, it was projected that the *Aquitania* would sail until 1940, when the new *Queen Elizabeth* would come into service and replace her. This plan went afoul when the Second World War erupted and the *Aquitania* was called to war duty—her second major conflict. After the hostilities, her position within the Cunard fleet was reappraised. She was given a reprieve of sorts and sailed in an austerity service between Southampton and Halifax with emigrants and troops and their families until 1949. In 1950, she was broken up in Scotland, not far from the place on the River Clyde where she had been built.

BERENGARIA.

The *Berengaria*, one of the most celebrated North Atlantic liners of the twenties and thirties, had two noteworthy distinctions. She had not been built for the company and she had not been named after one of the Roman provinces, as had been done previously. In May 1912, she had been launched as the *Imperator* by the German Kaiser. Then the largest and finest member of the ever-expanding Hamburg-America Line fleet (far larger than Cunard, for example, and with over 400 ships of all kinds by 1914), this liner—the world's largest, known as "the colossus" of the North Atlantic—was also the flagship of the Imperial German fleet. When she set off from Hamburg to New York for the first time, in the spring of 1913, the public was intrigued by her amazing details: 4,594 passengers in all, 83 lifeboats, a 90-ton rudder and a columned, two-deck-high indoor swimming pool, known as the Pompeian Bath and larger than the pool at London's Royal Automobile Club.

The *Imperator* was also the first of three successively larger liners that were intended to place Imperial Germany in the forefront of international shipping. If she was over 52,000 tons, the second ship, the *Vaterland*, would be 54,000 and the third, the *Bismarck*, would be 56,000. Cunard's largest at that time was the 45,000-ton *Aquitania*, while White Star's was 48,000-ton *Britannic*. The eruption of the First World War changed all this, however, and, in defeat, the Germans lost their mighty trio. Each of them was seized in reparations: The *Imperator* went to Cunard in compensation for the *Lusitania*; the *Vaterland* hoisted American colors and became the *Leviathan*; and the *Bismarck* joined White Star and became their *Majestic*, replacing the *Britannic*.

At first, this ship sailed for the Americans on troop duty as the U.S.S. *Imperator*. Then she was chartered to Cunard for temporary "austerity" service in 1919–20. Later, she formally joined Cunard and, in April 1921, became the *Berengaria*, being named after the wife of Richard the Lion-Heart. She began on Cunard's new express service out of Southampton, rather than the "fast ship" terminal previously used at Liverpool, and also became the company flagship, despite her well-known German origin. Almost from the start, she settled down to a very popular and successful career, and was soon affectionately dubbed "the Berry."

It was a special occasion when the world's largest and most luxurious ships went into dry dock at Southampton. Special excursion trains left London's Waterloo Station, often for a fare of less than £1. The British public, especially those unlikely to travel aboard the great transatlantic liners, had the opportunity to tour these "floating cities," sometimes while they were resting in dry dock, which made them appear larger still. Occasionally, day-trippers were even invited on board for a walk through the vast, fantasylike public rooms and the "miles" of corridors and perhaps even for afternoon tea in the restaurant. In this scene, tugs assist the giant *Berengaria* on January 17, 1934 into the special floating dock at Southampton. The dock served all of the big liners, but would be eclipsed that same month by the even larger King George V Graving Dock. Two days after the *Berengaria*'s docking, White Star's *Majestic* became the first ship to use the new graving dock. This new facility was created for the forthcoming construction of the largest British liners of all, the *Queen Mary* and the *Queen Elizabeth*. [Built by Bremer Vulkan Shipyards, Hamburg, Germany, 1913. 52,226 gross tons; 919 feet long; 98 feet wide; 38-foot draft. Steam turbines, quadruple screw. Service speed 23 knots. 2,723 passengers (972 first class, 630 second class, 606 third class, 515 tourist class).]

The Berengaria. The mighty foremast of the *Berengaria (above, left),* has two crow's nests. Since she was the first ship ever to exceed 50,000 gross tons, her designers thought big in every dimension. This close-up gives a marvelous view of the ratlines, retained even though there was plenty of room within the huge steel mast for a ladder reaching all the way up to the second crow's nest. Cargo booms are left and right of the mast proper. Many smaller liners boasted that they carried only passengers, not cargo. This was rarely true. The big German liners built by Ballin had large garages for the automobiles of their wealthy passengers—giant Pierce Arrows, huge Buicks and foreign cars, usually made to order for rich American buyers.

The *Berengaria*'s three huge funnels *(above, right),* which sometimes gave her a slight resemblance to the *Queen Mary*, were a matter of great concern in her earlier years. On her first voyages for Hamburg-America, she suffered from serious stability problems. The Germans added tons of cement to her bottom, removed all of the heavy marble from the interiors, and many of the ponderous chairs and sofas, and even cut the three towering funnels down by nine feet. Although this reduction improved the ship's overall appearance, in her Cunard days, beginning in 1921, stability remained a problem. The Liverpool engineers ordered more cement laid along the bottom.

A photograph of the *Berengaria*'s funnels, taken in September 1936, shows the considerable number of "guys," the wires that secured the funnels. The thin black band near the top of the funnel reveals how much of the original stack had to be cut off to correct her list.

The *Berengaria.* In a view of lower Manhattan, the *Berengaria* is seen outbound in the lower Hudson. Several commuting ferries, sailing to Jersey City, make their relays.

The *Berengaria*. An outside first-class cabin on B deck *(above)* was typical of liners in the twenties and early thirties. The bed—not a bunk—is made of steel. Lifejackets are tucked into a compartment on the wall. The small brass plate contains the call buttons for steward and stewardess. The sink, positioned between the two beds, consists of a marble-topped wood cabinet. The Art Deco wall covering seems to have been a later addition, and the bulb above the mirror is exposed. In the mid-thirties, peak-season passage to Southampton in this room was $160.

Until the mid-thirties, Cunard's main passenger terminal at New York was at the Chelsea Docks, Piers 53, 54 and 56, located between West 13 and West 15 Streets. But in 1936, the giant *Queen Mary*, a ship that was far too large for these piers, was assigned farther uptown to specially built Pier 90, at West 50 Street. Most Cunarders eventually moved to those docks. The new piers became known as "Luxury Liner Row." Smaller Cunard passenger ships did, however, continue to berth at the Chelsea Docks until the early 1950s.

In an aerial view *(opposite)*, the mighty *Berengaria*, having just returned from a short cruise, is being manuevered into the south slip of Pier 54. The equally large *Majestic*, part of the Cunard–White Star merger of 1934, is already berthed and farther to the left is the Anchor liner *Transylvania*, then another Cunarder, the *Lancastria*.

The Berengaria. A view taken from the port-side wing of the stern docking bridge *(opposite, top left)* shows the great height of the *Berengaria*. She is at sea, steaming southward on a short cruise to Bermuda. An advertisement of 1932 read:

Cap Haitien, Cartagena, Curaçao, San Juan, St Pierre, Barbados, Port of Spain, La Guaira, Nassau, St Thomas, Santo Domingo, Port au Prince, Fort de France, Havana. Magic, romantic, exciting names . . . on Cunard's unusual West Indies itineraries this season . . . Cap Haitien, famous during the reign of his Black Majesty, Christophe . . . Cartagena, Metropolis of the Spanish Main . . . are but two of the hidden, almost inaccessible ports that are yours to enjoy.

Lavish entertainments . . . deck sports . . . dances . . . and don't forget to come prepared for the costume party.

California	January 23rd	18 days	$185 up
Berengaria	February 11th	4 days	$50 up
California	February 13th	18 days	$185 up
Scythia	February 27th	23 days	$225 up
California	March 5th	15 days	$155 up
Scythia	April 16th	12 days	$120 up

And, beginning Friday, January 15th, the transatlantic liners *Scythia* and *Samaria*, by far the largest steamers in the Havana Service, sail alternately every Friday from New York to Nassau and Havana . . . returning 9 days later. Rates $90 one way, $125 roundtrip. No passports required.

The *Berengaria* was far too large to enter the harbor at Bermuda, and her cruise passengers, like those on the larger cruise ships today, had to be taken ashore in tenders. She is seen *(opposite, top right)* from the tender *Woodside* in September 1936. The five rectangular windows, just below the promenade deck, mark the lovely veranda of the famous Kaiser's Suite.

A shipboard afternoon *(opposite, bottom)* featured a comfortable deck chair, a good book, perhaps a nap and all the while a gentle breeze floating in through the *Berengaria's* promenade-deck windows. The scene is from a four-and-a-half-day cruise to Bermuda in September 1936. A little Sherlock Holmes sleuthing can be done with this photograph. We know the camera was pointed aft because the glass-enclosed promenade was on the forward half of the upper-promenade deck. The sun is streaming onto the teak deck and up the white steel bulkheads, indicating that it was coming in over the port side at about 3 P.M. For this to be happening, the liner must have been heading home from Bermuda, or have been more or less on a westward course.

A leisurely afternoon of fun and games during a cruise in July 1932: Two hooded passengers entertain others with a humorous boxing match *(above)*. The event was staged in the aft section of the *Berengaria*. The Depression forced Cunard to seek new markets to fill their ships. Most of these people had probably never sailed before.

The *Berengaria*. In a 1936 view, the *Berengaria* anchors off Five Fathom Hole at St. George. The passengers are going ashore for shopping, swimming and bicycling on beautiful Bermuda. In their absence, the ship will be quiet, her lounges, corridors and decks deserted. The staff will attend to cleaning and small repairs. Then, by late afternoon and early evening, the ship will again become the great floating hotel—cabins occupied, busy corridors, drinks in the bar and then the call to dinner.

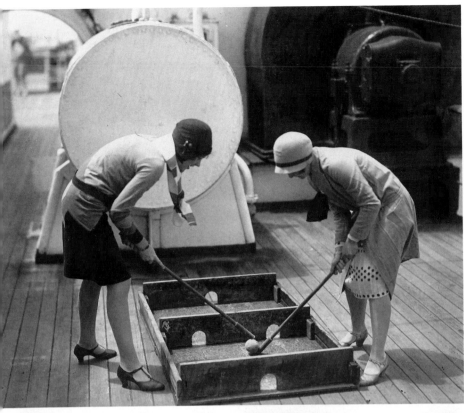

MAURETANIA.

The North Atlantic passage often had inclement weather—gray, overcast skies; rains and strong winds; sometimes sinister fogs. In winter, storms could be ferocious—full-scale blizzards and treacherous seas. But on tropical cruises, the voyage was often tranquil, sometimes like sailing on "a sheet of glass," from start to finish. In a view from the early thirties (*above*), two passengers enjoy the outdoors and one of the simpler amenities of the *Mauretania*. The women are models, and the photograph comes from an album salvaged by Frank Braynard when the Cunard New York office, moving uptown from 25 Broadway, discarded much archival material.

Don't be fooled by the White Star lettering on the gangway in the photograph on the left. The full wording was "Cunard–White Star"; the photo was made after the forced merger of the two famous British lines. Visitors disembark from the *Mauretania*, which is about to sail on a Caribbean cruise. A 1931 advertisement for one of these Depression-era cruises read:

> Cunard again does the unusual. The world-famous *Mauretania* in all its splendor and distinction . . . now at your service for West Indies cruises. A travel opportunity of unprecedented value. Spend Thanksgiving Day in Havana . . . via the *Mauretania*. She sails from New York on November 19th, stopping first at Bermuda and Nassau; December 3rd is her next sailing for the same ports. 10 happy, glorious days, and what value for your money! Inclusive rates as low as $140!

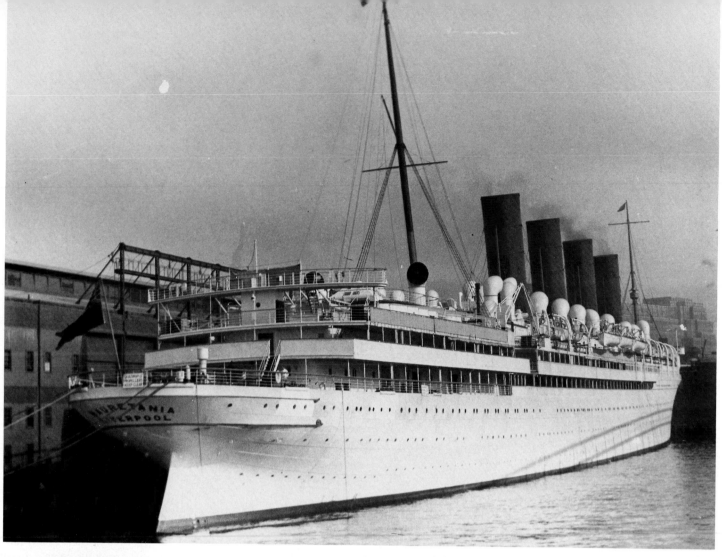

The Mauretania. In the bleakest Depression years, even the great *Mauretania*, still legendary and still well remembered as the Blue Ribbon champion for over two decades, was repainted white for extended heat resistance *(above)* and detoured to the tropics. Now, instead of her regular runs between New York and Southampton, she sailed (often at far slower speeds) to Nassau, Havana and Port-au-Prince.

The Depression, the advent of such new express ships as the *Queen Mary* and their own age spelled the end for several of the most illustrious Cunarders. Although the ships were beloved by the dockers, the shipyard crews, the baggage handlers and the taximen, there were fewer and fewer passengers. The older ships had to go. Following the Cunard–White Star merger in early 1934, creating a combined fleet, and then the impending arrival of the new *Queen Mary*, all of those older express liners were placed on the disposal list.

The white-hulled *Mauretania* (three of her funnels shown to the left in her twilight days) was the first to go. Following her final summer cruises, she left New York on September 26, 1934 (the same day that the *Queen Mary* was launched at Clydebank) for her last crossing. She was laid up for a time at Southampton and, by the following spring, the ship breakers had made an acceptable bid. In preparation, some of the ship's fittings were auctioned off—the chairs and sofas and tables, the mantelpieces, even wood paneling (some of which exists today in the Mauretania pub in Bristol).

Cunard had hoped to keep the aging *Berengaria* until 1940, when the new *Queen Elizabeth* was scheduled to enter service. The end came prematurely. She began to suffer an infirmity that often afflicts older liners: fires. Most were smaller outbreaks caused by outmoded, worn wiring systems. In 1936, there was a more serious blaze while she was berthed along the Southampton Docks; two years later, there was an even more alarming eruption at New York. United States authorities found her unsafe and revoked her sailing permit to carry American passengers. She returned empty to Southampton. While Cunard protested and denied the extent of her woes, a third fire occurred at her British berth. Her fate was sealed. She was sold to the breakers in October 1938, and dismantled at Jarrow. Dismantling was not completed until eight years later, when her double bottom was towed off to Rosyth and finally finished off.

THE INTERMEDIATES:
SINGLE-STACKERS OF THE TWENTIES

THE FIRST WORLD WAR had been especially cruel to Cunard, which lost 11 passenger ships: the *Lusitania*, the *Franconia*, the *Alaunia*, the *Ivernia*, the *Laconia*, the *Ultonia*, the *Andania*, the *Aurania*, the *Ausonia*, the *Carpathia* and the *Ascania*.

Restoring peacetime service was no easy task. The fleet survivors were an eclectic group: two express liners, the *Mauretania* and the *Aquitania*; the sisters *Caronia* and *Carmania*; and then three ships of dubious value, the *Saxonia*, the *Pannonia* and the *Royal George*, the last-named having been bought in 1916, when Cunard acquired the Canadian Northern Steamship Company. But far more berths were needed on the already hard-pressed North Atlantic.

In 1919–20, Cunard chartered a diverse group of passenger ships, some for only one or two voyages and others for a dozen or more. There was tonnage from several well-known British shippers: Union Castle, Pacific Steam Navigation and Lamport & Holt. Even P&O's crack London-to-Bombay express liner, the *Kaisar-I-Hind*, was chartered. She was advertised, however, under the English translation of her name, *Emperor of India*. Even a Dutch ship, the *Prinses Juliana*, and two war prizes, the big Germans *Kaiserin Auguste Victoria* and *Imperator*, were used. The *Imperator*, of course, remained with the Cunard fleet to become the *Berengaria*.

The Liverpool directors and designers had busy days ahead in planning new replacement tonnage. With the express run to New York already in hand with the *Mauretania*, the *Aquitania* and the *Berengaria*, Cunard wanted to reinforce its auxiliary services, not only to New York, but to Boston, Halifax and on the seasonal trade on the St. Lawrence to Quebec City and Montreal. It also wanted ships of moderate size—more practical, useful and economic. After all, with the age of mass North Atlantic immigration to America about to drop drastically (new American quotas were imposed in 1922), these ships would have to rely more and more on tourists and on those first-class passengers who wanted luxury, but not necessarily aboard the big floating palaces. And so, Cunard embarked on a very ambitious postwar rebuilding program—14 new passenger ships in all.

There was one "misfit" in the group, the *Albania* of 1920. She was the least successful. She was followed by a group of five: three identical sisters (the long-lived *Scythia* of 1921 and the *Samaria* and *Laconia* of 1922) and two modified sisters (the *Franconia* of 1923 and the *Carinthia* of 1925). The *Tyrrhenia*, a modified version of this group that had actually been ordered by the rival Anchor Line back in 1914, was also completed in 1922. Her name was soon changed to *Lancastria*. The design of the 20,000-ton *Scythia* class was then reworked, changed and reduced to the six sisters of the 14,000-ton "A Class"—the *Antonia*, the *Ausonia* and the *Andania* (1922), and then the *Aurania*, the *Ascania* and the *Alaunia* (1924–25).

These were Cunard's "intermediates"—their single-stackers of the twenties.

ALBANIA—A MISFIT (above).

It was perhaps only due to the severe shortage of adequate passenger tonnage that Cunard finished the four-masted *Albania*, a ship already dated by the time of her completion in January 1921. She had been planned before the war, and her very limited accommodation was only offset by a large cargo capacity. Her sailings, for example, could not be effectively coordinated with any other ship in the fleet—she was too small for the passenger runs yet too big for the freighter operations. She was a "lame duck." While she worked the Liverpool–New York route for a time and later entered the Canadian service, she had an extremely brief Cunard career, sailing for less than five years. She was laid up in the fall of 1925, the company designers evidently feeling that she was unworthy of being rebuilt. She lay idle for nearly five years before, at the very onset of the Depression, being sold to the Italians to become the *California*. She was later an early casualty of the Second World War. [Built by Scott's Shipbuilding & Engineering Company, Greenock, Scotland, 1920. 12,768 gross tons; 539 feet long; 64 feet wide. Steam turbines, twin screw. Service speed 13 knots. 80 cabin-class passengers, later expanded to 480.]

SCYTHIA—FIRST OF THE INTERMEDIATES (opposite, top).

The *Scythia* was the forerunner of this intermediate fleet of Cunarders, all of which were distinguished by having a single stack. She was laid down in 1919, immediately after the war, but her British construction was so beset by labor strikes that she had to be completed at Rotterdam. With three classes of accommodation, she was to reopen the trade from Liverpool and Queenstown (later renamed Cobh), Ireland, to New York and Boston. The *Scythia*'s passenger quarters, particularly in cabin class, were praised. The garden lounge, for example, was fitted with lush greenery; the oval lounge was capped by a domed skylight and the gymnasium was said to be among the best on the North Atlantic. There were also such novelties as the American bar (a very popular attraction with Prohibition-struck American travelers) and private bathrooms in most cabin-class staterooms (a feature rare in the twenties—even for some of the largest, most lavish liners).

The *Scythia* had a full life with Cunard as a wartime trooper (and survivor of an aerial torpedo attack), a postwar immigrant and refugee ship and, finally, refurbished for the St. Lawrence trade (1951–57). She went to the breakers at Inverkeithing, Scotland, in early 1958. Having sailed for 37 years, she was the last of this intermediate group still in Cunard hands.

In this view, dating from the early thirties, the fine broadside lines of the *Scythia* are evident. She is inbound on the Hudson River, passing the lower Manhattan skyline. [Built by Vickers-Armstrong Shipbuilders Limited, Barrow-in-Furness, England, 1921. 19,730 gross tons; 624 feet long; 74 feet wide. Steam turbines, twin screw. Service speed 16 knots. 2,206 passengers (337 cabin class, 331 tourist class, 1,538 third class).]

SCYTHIA AND FRANCONIA (opposite, bottom).

Two of Cunard's intermediate single-stackers appear in this 1933 view of New York's Chelsea Docks, showing (left to right): the *California* of the Panama Pacific Line; a small American Merchant Line passenger–cargo ship, just barely visible as her small funnel gives off thick black smoke; the four-funnel *Olympic* of the White Star Line; the *Rex* of the Italian Line and, at the time, the latest speed champion of the Atlantic, the holder of the coveted Blue Ribbon; two small American Pioneer Line freighters; the French liner *Champlain*, an exceptionally modern liner that was a prelude to the giant *Normandie* of 1935; and, finally, the two Cunarders, the *Scythia* and the *Franconia*.

LACONIA (opposite, bottom).

Passengers began to prefer the intermediate liners, not only because of their crisp Cunard service, the leisurely qualities of an eight-to-ten-day crossing or their comparative intimacy. Their splendid decoration earned a reputation of its own. The *Laconia* was, while otherwise an identical sister to the slightly earlier *Scythia* and *Samaria*, one of the best decorated of these intermediate passenger ships. Her writing room, for example, was done in the Adam style, her main lounge in Queen Anne and the smoking room was made to resemble an old English inn (including a red-brick fireplace). But like all of this class, she was designed both for Atlantic services and tropical cruises, especially in the winter, when North Atlantic weather usually turned its worst and passenger loads slumped.

There were considerable changes in the 1930s, especially in the early years, when the Depression dealt its worst blows. And so, avoiding the lay-up of ships and the consequent layoff of their crews, ships such as the *Laconia* were sent on cruises, often from British ports, frequently for as little as £1 a day. There were trips to the Canaries, Portugal and West Africa; to the Mediterranean; and to Norway and the Baltic. Occasional luxury trips catered to 300 or 400 millionaires, such as the *Laconia*'s 52-day cruise to South America, on which she left from Liverpool in January 1938. In that one voyage, she logged an overall distance of more than 14,000 miles.

The *Laconia* was a casualty of the Second World War. Converted to an armed merchant cruiser in September 1939, and later to a troopship, she was torpedoed off West Africa in September 1942. At the time, she was carrying over 1,800 Italian prisoners-of-war and 900 others; 100 survived, all of whom were rescued by nearby Nazi submarines. The prisoners were given unexpected freedom; the crew members were sent to internment in Morocco. [Built by Swan, Hunter & Wigham Richardson Shipbuilders, Limited, Newcastle, England, 1921. 19,860 gross tons; 623 feet long; 73 feet wide. Steam turbines, twin screw. Service speed 16 knots. 2,180 passengers (340 cabin class, 340 tourist class, 1,500 third class).]

WAR DUTIES FOR THE *FRANCONIA* (left).

The glamour of midnight suppers on North Atlantic crossings or of the cruises to such exotic places as Bali or Bombay was dramatically eclipsed in the fateful summer of 1939. That September, the *Franconia* was repainted gray and outfitted to carry 3000 troops. Dispatched to Mediterranean waters, on October 5 she collided with another big British liner being used as a trooper, Royal Mail Lines' *Alcantara*. The Cunarder was soon repaired, but more danger lay ahead. The following June, she was hit in an air attack while on evacuation service off western France.

The *Franconia* was called to a special duty at the war's end. Some of her prewar luxury fittings were taken from storage while she was still a gray-hulled trooper, and she was again sent to the Mediterranean to await top-secret instructions. Ordered to Yalta in the Black Sea, she served as the floating headquarters for Winston Churchill and his staff during the historic Yalta Conference. A series of suites was arranged for the prime minister and some of his favorite personal effects were brought from London. A staff of over 100 accompanied him on board, including secretaries, typists, telegraphers and security guards. Since Cunard had already hosted Churchill on board the *Queen Mary* on several occasions it thought of the smallest details. Since the prime minister enjoyed soaking in the oversized tub, a special wooden shelf was erected so that he could attend to paperwork at the same time.

A SPECIAL PAIR (opposite, top).

The *Franconia*, completed in June 1923, and the *Carinthia*, delivered two summers later, were improved versions of the earlier *Scythia* class. There were differences in design and they were better decorated, more luxurious. While they were intended to run Liverpool–New York sailings, they were planned to cruise in winter. Even in the 1920s, Cunard saw tremendous potential in the future of cruising. Not only would there be $10-a-day short voyages out of New York to Bermuda, Nassau, Havana and other Caribbean ports, but also long, luxurious jaunts, such as eight weeks around South America, another cruise around Africa, tours of the Mediterranean and summer trips to Scandinavia. The world cruises of both the *Franconia* and *Carinthia* became legendary, particularly for 1930s travel. The *Franconia* developed a loyal following, one that included Cole Porter, Noël Coward, Richard Rodgers and Oscar Hammerstein. Many well-known songs and musical productions were at least inspired by the travels undertaken on this beloved Cunarder.

The *Franconia*'s quarters were splendid: a two-deck-high smoking room that was styled after the fifteenth-century residence of El Greco; another lounge done in Early English style; twin garden lounges; and such special amenities as a chocolate shop, health center and even a racquetball court.

In this unusual view taken June 24, 1932, three Cunarders sail on the Hudson River. The *Franconia* is outbound at the far left. The regal *Aquitania* is inbound at center and the *Mauretania* is outbound at the far right. It was far busier in New York harbor than today. In this photograph, there are nine tugs, six barges and three ferries. In the background is Manhattan's financial district. [Built by John Brown & Company Limited, Clydebank, Scotland, 1923. 20,158 gross tons; 623 feet long; 73 feet wide. Steam turbines, twin screw. Service speed 16.5 knots. 1,843 passengers (221 first class, 356 second class, 1,266 third class).]

The *Franconia* (*above*). Surviving the Second World War and, after a stint on postwar refugee and immigrant service, the ship was fully restored. Her berthing reduced considerably—to 253 in first class and 600 in tourist class—she was put on the Canadian service, from Liverpool and Greenock (Scotland) to Quebec City in summer, to Halifax in winter. She also sailed to New York. Her revived career was not without incident, however. On July 14, 1950, just a mile downriver from Quebec City, the liner went aground; with her advancing years, her steering gear had become faulty. The passengers were removed and sent to local hotels and whatever other accommodation might be available. But the ship remained tight in position. The crew was then asked to pack passenger belongings and other items to lighten the ship's load. In the end, it took a team of tugs and four days to free her. She returned to Quebec for temporary repairs and then crossed to Liverpool, where full repairs were made.

LANCASTRIA (*below*).

Completed as the *Tyrrhenia* in the summer of 1922, this Cunard intermediate differed in design and was, in fact, nearer to being a half-sister to the Anchor Line's *Cameronia*, having been designed for that firm just before the start of the First World War. She was transferred to Cunard after the armistice. Her Anchor name, never popular and hard to spell, was even disliked by the notorious Liverpool dockers. By 1924, she was renamed the *Lancastria*.

Hard hit in the lean 1930s, she obviated the possibility of lay-up by running bargain cruises out of New York and British ports, for which her hull was repainted white. Perhaps her most notable cruise came in May 1935, when she ran a six-day trip out of Liverpool that included participation in the enormous Silver Jubilee fleet review off Spithead for King George V. Officially, Cunard (by then Cunard–White Star) was represented by the giant *Berengaria* and the *Homeric*.

The *Lancastria*'s end was one of the most tragic in maritime history. Requisitioned as a trooper in the first bleak weeks of September 1939, she was later selected to participate in the evacuation of refugees from France, on June 17, 1940. As the French surrendered to the advancing Nazi forces, the *Lancastria* arrived at St. Nazaire and took on over 5,000 evacuees (including considerable numbers of women and children). Shortly afterward, she was attacked by enemy bombers. The first bomb went through her funnel and exploded in the engine room, and the two others fell into the cargo holds and blew out the sides of the ship. Survivors reported that the *Lancastria* seemed to jump out of the water. She sank within 20 minutes with the loss of over 3,000. The tragedy was considered by many, including Churchill himself, to be so demoralizing that full details were withheld for five years, until the first summer of peace in 1945. [Built by William Beardmore & Company, Glasgow, Scotland, 1922. 16,243 gross tons; 578 feet long; 70 feet wide; 30-foot draft. Steam turbines, twin screw. Service speed 16.5 knots. 1,846 passengers (235 first class, 355 second class, 1,256 third class).]

CARINTHIA (above).

Carrying as few as 400 passengers and later repainted a heat-resistant white, the *Franconia* and *Carinthia* resembled large white yachts. They were known everywhere for their luxurious world cruises. An advertisement for one of the first read:

> You'll want the best! The Raymond-Whitcomb Round the World Cruise. Sails from New York, October 10th 1925; from Los Angeles, October 25th; from San Francisco, October 27th. Visits Cuba, Panama, Hawaii, Japan, China, the Philippines, New Guinea, New Zealand, Australia, Java, Singapore, India, Egypt, Italy, France and England; European termination March 1st 1926, New York on March 10th. All on board the new 20,000-ton *Carinthia*. The route: the admittedly superior westbound course—sailing from the 51st degree north of the Equator to the 45th degree south—38,000 miles—149 days of cruising—visiting 51 ports and places of prime interest in 21 countries and colonies. The ship: the brand new *Carinthia*, finest of Cunarders—launched in 1925—unique equipment—instantaneous running hot water in every room used—beds six inches wider than on other ships—exceptional deck space—squashcourt and pool. All for $2,000 upward.

Here the *Carinthia* is shown at Cunard's Pier 90 in New York in the winter of 1937–38, when she was being used on weekly cruises to Nassau. She would become a war casualty, being torpedoed off the Irish Coast by a Nazi submarine in June 1940. [Built by Vickers Armstrong Shipbuilders, Limited, Barrow-in-Furness, England, 1925. 20,227 gross tons; 624 feet long; 73 feet wide. Steam turbines, twin screw. Service speed 16.5 knots. 1,650 passengers (240 first class, 460 second class, 950 third class).]

LANCASTRIA (right).

Built-in outdoor swimming pools did not become a regular feature of Atlantic liners until the thirties, when they were used on Mediterranean-bound ships. The northern-based ships, which often had to endure chilly and rainy weather, simply had no need for them. But, on occasion, when these ships went cruising to the tropics, a portable canvas pool was rigged, usually in the stern cargo section. This view from the twenties was taken when the *Lancastria* was bound for the Caribbean.

ANTONIA AND THE A CLASS (opposite, top).

The *Antonia* was the first of the so-called "A Class"—the *Antonia*, the *Andania* and the *Ausonia* (all 1922), and then extended by three more, the *Aurania*, the *Alaunia* and the *Ascania* (1924–25). Smaller than the earlier *Scythia* class, they were even more functional: a clear division between upper-deck cabin class and far more austere third class, and a large cargo capacity. The ideal little Atlantic liners, they could be moved about easily—summers to Quebec and Montreal, winters to Halifax and St. John or in the New York service. They soon established enviable reputations for their precision service and smart accommodations. On board the *Antonia*, for example, the cabin-class smoking room was done in Adam style, the lounge in Louis XIV style. The restaurant ran the full width of the ship.

In this striking photo of the *Antonia*, taken while she was on her sea trials in May 1922, the simple but pleasant lines of the A Class are evident. The single stack is canted slightly, the seven sets of lifeboats are nested in pairs and the tops of the king posts serve as ventilators. The counter stern, so common to passenger ships well through the 1920s, has a particular grace to it. [Built by Vickers-Armstrong Shipbuilders, Limited, Barrow-in-Furness, England, 1922. 13,867 gross tons; 540 feet long; 65 feet wide. Steam turbines, twin screw. Service speed 15 knots. 1,706 passengers (484 cabin class, 1,222 third class).]

AUSONIA (opposite, bottom).

The fates of the six A Class liners were remarkable, only the *Ascania* rejoining Cunard after the Second World War. The *Andania* was sunk by a German U-boat off Reykjavik, Iceland, in June 1940. But the irony concerns the other four. Because of a shortage of available wartime tonnage, all were sold to the British Admiralty, stripped thoroughly and then rebuilt as Royal Navy fleet-repair ships—floating workshops. The *Antonia* became the H.M.S. *Wayland* in 1944, and was scrapped four years later in Scotland. The *Ausonia* (shown departing from Cunard's West 14 Street pier in Manhattan in the late twenties) was relisted as H.M.S. *Ausonia* and served the fleet for some years at Malta. She was decommissioned in 1964, and broken up a year later in Spain. By then, nearly 45, she was the lone survivor of the original group. The *Aurania* became H.M.S. *Artifex* in 1944, and lasted until Italian scrappers bought her in 1961. Finally, the *Alaunia*, as H.M.S. *Alaunia*, finished her days in 1957 at Blyth in Scotland. [*Ausonia:* Built by Armstrong Whitworth Shipbuilders, Limited, Newcastle, England, 1921. 13,912 gross tons; 538 feet long; 65 feet wide. Steam turbines, twin screw. Service speed 15 knots. 1,688 passengers (510 cabin class, 1,178 third class).]

ALAUNIA (above).

Aside from bingo, the horse-racing game and an occasional concert after dinner, scheduled entertainment was unknown on most transatlantic liners, ships such as the *Alaunia* and her other A Class sisters being modes of transportation—not the floating hotels run by Cunard and others today. However, there were those occasions when entertainers wanted to travel to and from Europe and, in lieu of cash fares, offered their services for the duration of the crossing. In this view, a jazz band on its way to London has become, at least for the nine-day passage, "the Alaunians."

ASCANIA (left).

The *Ascania* served in the Second World War as a trooper, but did not become a repair ship as did her sisters. She was returned to Cunard in 1947, but only to run an austerity service with emigrants, refugees and servicemen and their families, between Liverpool and Halifax. Her companion at the time was none other than the *Aquitania*, also listed as an austerity ship. The *Ascania* was fully restored, however, in 1949–50. But times and requirements had certainly changed. Her prewar capacity of 500 in cabin class and 1,200 in third class had been cut down. She went on the Montreal service, with a trip to New York now and then, until she was broken up in 1957. Just before her date with the breakers, she had one last call to duty when she carried British servicemen to the Eastern Mediterranean during the Suez crisis. [Built by Armstrong Whitworth Shipbuilders, Limited, Newcastle, England, 1925. 14,440 gross tons; 538 feet long; 65 feet wide. Steam turbines, twin screw. Service speed 15 knots. 696 passengers (after 1950, 198 in first class and 498 in tourist class).]

CALEDONIA AND CUNARD-ANCHOR (opposite, top).

Cunard often coordinated its passenger services with other British-flag transatlantic firms. In the twenties and thirties, there was considerable cooperation between Liverpool-based Cunard and the Glasgow-headquartered Anchor Line, which maintained a small fleet of liners that were similar to Cunard's *Scythia* and the A Class ships. At times, Anchor liners would be included in Cunard sailing schedules and would use Cunard berths at New York. They would also appear in joint advertising. In January 1930, for example, a series of advertisements ran as:

The modern vacationist knows his below par season . . . therefore Cunard–Anchor West Indies cruises are appropriately scheduled:

January 6th 1930	*Carinthia*	16 days	$200 & up
January 16th	*Caledonia*	26 days	$275 & up
February 15th	*Caledonia*	26 days	$275 & up
March 15th	*Caledonia*	18 days	$200 & up
April 12th	*Samaria*	12 days	$175 & up

Connoisseurs appraised Anchor's *Caledonia* and her twin sister, the *Transylvania*, as two of the best-looking Atlantic liners. Although the first and third stacks were actually dummies, the three-funnel design was intended to give the ships added style by making them appear larger and reminding the public of the big Atlantic greyhounds.

In this view, the flag-bedecked *Caledonia* arrives at Halifax in June 1930. As the Depression set in, one-, two- and three-night cruises became increasingly popular. At $45 for a "long weekend to Nova Scotia," these were voyages of escape. [Built by Alexander Stephen & Sons Limited, Glasgow, Scotland, 1925. 17,046 gross tons; 552 feet long; 70 feet wide. Steam turbines, twin screw. Service speed 16 knots. 1,408 passengers (205 first class, 403 second class, 800 third class).]

CALIFORNIA (opposite, bottom).

Anchor's single-stackers—the *California* (shown departing from New York in 1932), the *Tuscania* and the *Cameronia*—resembled the intermediate Cunarders. They too ran on Cunard–Anchor joint sailings, the *Tuscania* actually being chartered by Cunard to run London–New York sailings between 1926 and 1931. Afterward, like so many other Atlantic liners, including almost all of the smaller Cunarders, she faced hard times. The *Tuscania* ran discount cruises, made seasonal trips to Bombay and was even chartered, in September 1934, to serve as a "floating grandstand" when she was positioned in Scotland's River Clyde, near the John Brown shipyards, for a very special occasion in British maritime history—the launching of the *Queen Mary*. [Built by Alexander Stephen & Sons Limited, Glasgow, Scotland, 1923. 16,792 gross tons; 579 feet long; 69 feet wide. Steam turbines, twin screw. Service speed 16 knots. 2,760 passengers (251 first class, 465 second class, 1,044 third class).]

The *California*. The Anchor liners were known for their immaculate qualities—"Everything glowed that was meant to glow, everything shined that was meant to shine." The cabin-class main lounge aboard the *California (left)* was a luxurious yet comfortable space, one that might have been found in a good British hotel or in a great country house. There were finely polished mahogany tables, oriental carpets, overstuffed sofas, a working fireplace and a grand piano tucked in the corner. Just footsteps away was the smoking room, but it might have been on board an entirely different ship, being done in 1920s moderne—blond woods, little detailing, simple furniture, plain carpeting and a new touch to shipboard design and decoration—indirect lighting.

Master photographer and ship-photograph collector Everett Viez took the view below from the uppermost deck of the *California* on July 26, 1937 at 11:30 PM. The ship is at Glasgow and the view ahead is of the River Clyde and its famed shipyards.

The California. This interesting view, taken by Everett Viez on July 27, 1937, catches the *California* at sea, en route from Glasgow and Londonderry to Boston and New York. Within little more than two years, with the outbreak of the Second World War, all Anchor transatlantic passenger services would be ended. The company did not reopen its New York liner routes afterward, running instead freighter services as Cunard–Anchor, usually on the "whiskey run" between Glasgow and New York.

MERGER:
CUNARD–WHITE STAR

THE EARLY THIRTIES COULD not have been worse for shipping, the North Atlantic having grown short of its most precious commodity—passengers. The Depression was felt worldwide. Passenger liners began to sail half-full, and sometimes even emptier, and were occasionally scarred with rust streaks, the result of "deferring" costly maintenance. Future prospects were bleak—the lay-up of ships and the layoff of their crews or, worse still, complete bankruptcy and collapse. Both Cunard and its nearest British transatlantic rival, the White Star Line (which had actually been owned by the American J. P. Morgan interests until the mid-twenties) were hard hit. Both firms suddenly found that they had too many ships and far too many berths.

Another pressing problem, however, was that both the Cunard and White Star express services were being run by aging superliners—the *Mauretania*, for example, was 23 by 1930. Company directors as well as the British government itself were rightfully worried. Continental firms were making important strides: The French had just added the stunning *Ile de France* and planned at least three more, including the ultraluxurious *Normandie;* the Germans were adding two greyhounds, the *Bremen* and the *Europa;* and even "those distant Italians" had twin superships on the boards. Britain needed to plan her retaliation to the competition.

Despite its increasing financial ills, in June 1928, White Star ordered its biggest liner yet, the 60,000-ton *Oceanic*. She was intended to break records, including being the first liner to exceed 1,000 feet in length, and would cost a hefty £3.5 million. Simultaneously, Cunard designers planned an even bigger ship, a projected 75,000-tonner (actually completed in excess of 81,000 tons), the illustrious *Queen Mary*. Inevitably, the two ships would have been teamed.

But the *Oceanic* was never to be. Within 13 months of the start of her construction at Belfast, the increasingly fragile White Star Company was forced to cancel the order and the small skeleton was cut up. But all was not lost. White Star had also ordered, from the same Belfast builders, a more moderate-sized "cabin liner," the *Britannic*. The *Oceanic*'s cancellation was later being altered to an order for a sister "cabin liner," the *Georgic*, the last White Star passenger liner. By the end of 1930, White Star, which had started its passenger services in 1871, posted losses of nearly £400,000. Worse times were ahead. Passenger lists dropped by nearly a quarter of a million by late 1931.

Both Cunard and White Star needed help, although the latter was far more vulnerable. The British government was called upon, an inquiry was arranged and, as a result, House of Commons passed the North Atlantic Shipping Act in 1933. It authorized a loan of £9.5 million to Cunard and White Star—divided as £3 million to complete the *Queen Mary* (then still enduring a near two-year delay at Clydeside), £5 million toward a running mate (the *Queen Elizabeth* of 1940) and £1.5 million working capital, provided the two companies merged. And so, on January 1, 1934, Cunard–White Star, Limited was formed, a name that would remain in use until 1950 and whose last ship, the *Britannic*, was in service until 1960.

In this marriage of rivals, Cunard—with 15 liners of its own—acquired another ten passenger ships, including what was then the largest in the world, the 56,500-ton *Majestic*. But, as the Depression lingered and as the Atlantic trade barely improved, disposals—and most of them from White Star—became the order of the day.

MAJESTIC.

The *Majestic*, affectionately dubbed the "Magic Stick" by fond passengers, crew and dockers, was the premier ship in the White Star fleet in 1934. She was the world's largest liner, a prized distinction she held from 1922 until the debut, in spring 1935, of the French *Normandie*, a 79,000-tonner.

The *Majestic* had been ordered by the Hamburg-America Line just before the start of the First World War as part of a three-ship set, the others being the *Imperator* (later Cunard's *Berengaria*) and the *Vaterland* (which became the American *Leviathan*). The *Majestic*, originally named the *Bismarck*, was to be the largest. She was so popular that she was scheduled to take the Kaiser and the imperial family on an around-the-world celebratory cruise after the anticipated

German victory. Of course, the Germans lost the war, the Kaiser went into exile and the *Bismarck* went to a reparations committee that finally awarded her to the White Star Line as the replacement for the 48,000-ton *Britannic*, lost to a mine in 1916, when only a year old. When she was finally commissioned under British colors in spring 1922, the *Majestic* was accorded the honor of a special visit by King George V and Queen Mary. Throughout the twenties and into the early thirties, the *Majestic* was regularly teamed with the *Olympic* and the *Homeric* on White Star's express run. [Built by Blohm & Voss Shipbuilders, Hamburg, Germany, 1914–22. 56,551 gross tons; 956 feet long; 100 feet wide; 38-foot draft. Steam turbines, quadruple screw. Service speed 23.5 knots. 2,145 passengers (750 first class, 545 second class, 850 third class).]

The *Majestic*. In January 1934, King George V and Queen Mary opened the new graving dock at Southampton and the first ship to use it was, quite appropriately, the world's largest, the mighty *Majestic*. It was a tremendous spectacle—the merging of shoreside engineering genius with a floating marvel. Actually, it was the first time that the liner could be overhauled in home waters. Previously, because of her great size, she had to go each winter to the Boston Naval Shipyard. The new dock, created especially for the coming *Queen Mary* and *Queen Elizabeth*, was named the King George V Graving Dock.

But the *Majestic*, seen here in New York during the summer of 1926, was not immune to trouble. In September 1934, for example, she encountered such a huge North Atlantic wave that tons of water all but flooded her upper decks and her master was so injured that the staff captain had to assume command.

The *Majestic*. The ship's main lounge *(opposite, top)* was her largest public room. A spectacular space, it was described in White Star advertising literature:

> Lofty, spacious, dignified, the *Majestic*'s lounge is distinguished by its perfect symmetry, unbroken by bays, projections or roof supports; by the substantial beauty of its oak-panelled walls with their hand-carved ornamentation; by its tall French windows admitting floods of sunshine; by the richness of the ceiling of crystal and carved wood in which concealed lights at night throw the florid dark carving into bold relief, striking a keynote of beauty.

White Star promotional literature reported that the *Majestic*'s passenger interiors were equivalent to 400 eight-room houses. The columned indoor pool, done in Pompeian style, had a full depth of almost ten feet. The domed-ceiling dining room *(opposite, bottom)*, surely one of the largest at sea at the time, could accommodate almost 700 at one seating.

OLYMPIC *(above)*.

White Star publicists went to considerable lengths to avoid reminders that the *Olympic* was actually an earlier sister of the ill-fated *Titanic*.

For the most part, she had a charmed life and was certainly one of the most popular of Atlantic liners. She was dubbed "Old Reliable" by the troops that sailed in her in the First World War. Her wartime record included a heroic attempt to tow a stricken battleship to safety and the sinking of a German U-boat. But in her career, there were less auspicious events: In September 1912 she collided with a British cruiser and in May 1934 she sank the Nantucket Lightship off New York.

In the lean years of the early thirties, the *Olympic* was among those hardest hit. She often arrived at New York as in this view, taken in April 1931) with as few as 500 passengers. In the end, she was sent on £1-a-day Bank Holiday cruises from Southampton and on three-day trips up to Halifax from New York. Deficit-ridden, she was laid up in the spring of 1935. While the Italians eyed her for possible use as a troopship in their East African campaigns, British ship breakers bought her instead. [Built by Harland & Wolff Limited, Belfast, Northern Ireland, 1911. 46,439 gross tons; 882 feet long; 92 feet wide. Steam triple expansion engines, triple screw. Service speed 21 knots. 1,447 passengers in 1932 (618 first class, 447 tourist class, 382 third class).]

HOMERIC.

The *Homeric* had been ordered as the *Columbus*, for the North German Lloyd in 1913. (A sister, the intended *Hindenburg*, was retained by the Germans and was completed as a "second" *Columbus*.)

In 1919, after reparations, White Star sent a team of designers and engineers to Danzig to supervise the ship's completion. In service by February 1922, she soon became the third part of White Star's "Big Three," the others being the *Majestic* and the *Olympic*. But the *Homeric* (seen here in Naples) needed an identiy of her own, and at first the publicity agents were stumped. But then her sound design and construction created a reputation for her as one of the "steadiest liners on the Atlantic."

Regrettably, the beautifully appointed *Homeric* had a comparatively short career on the New York run—a little less than ten years. In June 1932, because of the Depression, she was among the first liners to be used for full-time cruising, usually running two-week trips from Southampton and Liverpool to the Canaries, West Africa and into the Mediterranean. She had a superb reputation to rely on for these trips, having developed a secondary role as a deluxe winter cruise ship in the twenties. But, in the end, even these shorter cruises did not make enough profit. One of her last tasks was to help represent Cunard–White Star during King George V's Silver Jubilee fleet review off Spithead, on July 16, 1935. Two months later, she was laid up permanently. In better times, she might have been sold; instead she went to the breakers at Inverkeithing in Scotland the following year. In all, she had seen only 13 years of service. [Built by Schichau Shipyards, Danzig, Germany, 1913–22. 34,352 gross tons; 774 feet long; 82 feet wide; 36-foot draft. Steam triple expansion engines, twin screw. Service speed 19 knots. 2,766 passengers (529 first class, 487 second class, 1,750 third class).]

ADRIATIC.

They were known as the "Big Four"—two sets of sisters, the *Celtic* (1901) and the *Cedric* (1903), and the *Baltic* (1904) and the *Adriatic* (1907). All but the *Adriatic* were, for short periods, the world's largest liners. In their time, they were the crack ships of the White Star fleet and, as exemplified by the rather dated look created by the four tall masts, they were intended to remind the public of the glorious sailing ships of the previous century. They were unpretentious and very conservative—comfortable and sound, never intended to break speed records or skimp on passenger ease. They worked the Liverpool–New York trade, with a weekly sailing in each direction. The White Star express service was moved to Southampton in 1911 with the arrival of the *Olympic*, the first of the new three-ship team.

Each of the "Big Four" survived the ordeals of the First World War to resume White Star sailings throughout the twenties. The *Celtic* was stranded near Cobh, Ireland, in December 1928. After all salvage attempts failed, she was declared a constructive loss. Sold to Danish salvagers, her wreckage was not fully cleared until 1933. The *Cedric, Baltic* and *Adriatic* soon faced hard times and were among the

first victims of the Depression within the White Star fleet. The *Cedric* went to Scottish ship breakers in January 1932, her sale price of just over £22,000 being needed to help restore the failing coffers of the White Star Company. A year later, with the Japanese offering better prices in the scrap market, the *Baltic* left Liverpool under her own steam and was delivered to demolition crews at Osaka. The *Adriatic*, the lone survivor of this quartet at the time of the Cunard–White Star merger early in 1934, was already on the disposal lists. She spent her final season on inexpensive cruises, often under charter to the British Boy Scouts Association. That November, she was laid up for good. With the Japanese scrap market still offering attractive prices, she too went east. She was handed over at Osaka in March 1935, the oldest of the original White Star fleet—a company that seemed to be losing almost all of its ships rapidly. [Built by Harland & Wolff, Limited, Belfast, Northern Ireland, 1907. 24,541 gross tons; 726 feet long; 75 feet wide. Steam quadruple expansion engines, twin screw. Service speed 17 knots. 1,470 passengers by 1934 (506 cabin class, 560 tourist class, 404 third class).]

CHANGING FUNNELS.

The 1930s was a period of transition in ocean-liner design. A new breed of sleeker, smarter, more raked ships appeared while many of the older, statelier, far more conservative ones remained. Funnels have always been an intriguing part of a ship and certainly are among the most recognizable feature. In this quartet of photographs—all of them taken by Everett Viez—a comparison can be made. All the views, from the early thirties, were taken at New York's Chelsea piers. The *Adriatic* (1907; *above, top*) clearly shows the older design: two pencil-thin, very tall funnels. The four stacks of the *Olympic* (1911; *above, bottom*) represent the "big ship" era, when four funnels meant that a ship was stronger and safer, and therefore lured more

passengers, particularly those in steerage. The three funnels of the *Majestic* (1914–22; *opposite, top*) hint of a more modern approach, the three funnels accommodating more top-deck space. Strides in below-deck venting had also taken place. No longer were the exhaust shafts run straight up to the funnels; instead, they were arranged along the sides of the ship (providing for unobstructed public rooms). The squat stacks of the "motorship era" hint of the streamlined age of the 1930s. Ships such as Germany's *Bremen*, the British *Alcantara* and the Dutch *Johan van Oldenbarnevelt* were among the others that had the same racy look as the *Georgic* (*opposite, bottom*). On board this White Star liner, however, only the second stack was used; the forward one was a dummy that housed the engineers' lounge.

BRITANNIC.

Motorliners came into vogue in the late twenties. Diesel propulsion was more efficient than the steam turbines, and some believed that it gave an even smoother performance. Certainly, a number of the world's most important shippers, White Star among them, gave these "diesel ships" serious consideration. After leaving J. P. Morgan's International Mercantile Marine Group in the mid-twenties, and before the merger with Cunard in 1934, White Star was part of a consortium of British liner companies, the Royal Mail Group. Their management believed strongly in motorships. There was also an increasing fascination with so-called "cabin liners," ships that had cabin class instead of first class as their premium space. This meant comfort and luxury, but at lower, second-class fares. It was yet another attempt to lure more passengers.

Thus, when White Star decided on a new liner in 1928, it was decided that she would be a motorship as well as a "cabin liner." In fact, when she was finished in June 1930, the new Britannic ranked as the largest and fastest motorliner in the British merchant fleet. (Ironically, in 1927, White Star added the 19,000-ton Laurentic; years behind in design, she was a coal-burner that used prewar-style triple expansion engines.) The Britannic was an extreme change. The new ship's builders emphasized that she was among the most economical

liners of her day, using far less fuel oil than most comparable liners.

The Britannic had the long, almost lean look of the "thirties motorship." Her superstructure seemed comparatively low, her masts tall and raked, and her funnels squat and canted (the forward one being a dummy that served as a wireless room). Her whistles had an unusual placement on the second, aft stack and on the forward mast. One dated detail in her overall design was the use of old-fashioned quadrant davits for her lifeboats. It was surprising that her owners and builders did not use the newer gravity types.

The interior of the Britannic, as seen in the cabin-class lounge (opposite, top), made her one of the more contemporary liners of the early thirties. She had definite Art Deco touches—lighter woods, inlaid wood floors, simple burl columns, chromium-encased light fixtures and carpeting incorporating swirls and dramatic patterns.

In 1939, this cabin-class (the alternate to first-class) stateroom for two (opposite, bottom) was priced at $244 each on a peak summertime crossing from New York to London. Forced-air vents are on the left, a fan on the right. [Built by Harland & Wolff, Limited, Belfast, Northern Ireland, 1930. 26,943 gross tons; 712 feet long; 82 feet wide. Burmeister & Wain diesels, twin screw. Service speed 18 knots. 1,553 passengers (504 cabin class, 551 tourist class, 498 third class).]

The Britannic. A view of the promenade-deck cocktail lounge *(opposite, top)* taken after the Second World War features decorative linen-fold paneling and heraldic details. The furniture, of brown oak covered in leather and tapestry of the Hungarian point design, was taken from the *Aquitania*, whose furnishings had been stored in 1939. Then, since she was not refitted for luxury service in the late forties, the furnishings were sent instead to the renewed *Britannic*. Some of the *Aquitania*'s carpets also found their way aboard this White Star ship.

While her near-sister, the *Georgic*, tended to be more modern, more obviously of the Art Deco age, the *Britannic* was a more conservative ship. For example, on the port side of her aft funnel casing, a 90-foot-long gallery *(opposite, bottom)* led to the ship's main lounge, which was done to resemble an eighteenth-century English room.

The cabin-class dining room *(above)* rose two decks in the center and ran the full width of the ship. Indirect lighting illuminated the center of the room; the lower section had lights shining through opaque-glass sconces. It is easy to see why the *Britannic* and the *Georgic* were among the most popular liners of the thirties.

GEORGIC.

The *Britannic* had originally been ordered alone, but after cancellation of the giant *Oceanic* in the summer of 1929, a near-sister was also ordered. Arriving in June 1932, she was slightly larger than the *Britannic* and incorporated some design modifications, the most noticeable being that her forward superstructure was rounded, making it seem sleeker than the squared-off superstructure of the *Britannic*. The *Georgic* was the last White Star liner to be built, marking the end of the company's long association with the master shipbuilders, Harland & Wolff of Belfast (where she is seen above, being fitted out in the spring of 1932).

Because of their lower fares in cabin class, the improved comforts in their tourist-class and especially in their third-class sections (one-way costing as little as £19 in 1935) and because they were "new" ships (the newest Atlantic liners always had special appeal), both the *Britannic* and the *Georgic* were among the most successful liners of the Cunard–White Star fleet. At one point, the *Britannic* actually carried more passengers than any other liner in the company's fleet. Initially used on the Liverpool–New York service, in 1935 they were switched to the London run, becoming the largest liners to use that port regularly. Both ships also did considerable cruising: $100 for eight days to Bermuda and Nassau, $210 for 18 days to the Caribbean and $660 for 42 days to the Mediterranean.

During the Second World War, the *Britannic* and *Georgic* were used as troopers, the latter very nearly becoming a casualty. On July 14, 1941, the *Georgic*, painted gray, was at Egypt's Port Tewfik during a Nazi air raid. She caught fire and her own fans and blowers spread the blaze and smoke throughout her interior. In the end, she was a badly blistered shell of a ship. Few thought she could ever be repaired. But because of the urgent need for all ships, especially big troopers, in the war effort, she was temporarily patched and towed by two British freighters to Port Sudan. Further progress was slow. In March 1942, she was moved to Karachi; that December, she was at Bombay; finally, she was returned to Belfast for total repairs and rebuilding. She returned to action in December 1944, a far different ship. The effects of the fire were still evident—twisted beams, misshapen steel panels, the removal of the forward dummy stack. There were very few reminders of her Cunard–White Star luxury days. She was dubbed "the corrugated lung" by her crew. [Built by Harland & Wolff, Limited, Belfast, Northern Ireland, 1932. 27,759 gross tons; 711 feet long; 82 feet wide. Burmeister & Wain diesels, twin screw. Service speed 18 knots. 1,542 passengers (479 cabin class, 557 tourist class, 506 third class).]

SWAN SONG OF THE *MAJESTIC*.

In the fading light of a winter afternoon, in the mid-thirties, the *Majestic* leaves her New York berth on one of her final crossings, only a few hundred passengers on board. Since there were still too few passengers on the Atlantic for far too many ships, the new joint Cunard–White Star management had decided to dispose of almost all White Star tonnage, with the obvious exception of the two newest, the *Britannic* and the *Georgic*. Others included the *Albertic* (18,900 tons, scrapped 1934), the *Laurentic* (18,700 tons, used as a troopship and then laid up before being torpedoed in 1940), the *Doric* (16,400 tons, broken up in 1935 after a serious collision) and the *Calgaric* (16,000 tons, scrapped 1934).

The *Majestic*, now third largest liner, having been surpassed by the new *Queen Mary* and the French Line's *Normandie*, was retired in February 1936. At first, she was laid up along the Southampton Docks, only showing signs of life when she was dressed up in flags for the maiden reception of the *Queen Mary* that spring. In May she was sold to Scottish scrappers at Inverkeithing for £115,000. Her tall masts and funnels were trimmed to allow clear passage under the Forth Railway Bridge. Then, suddenly, there seeemed to be a chance for renewed life. The British Admiralty needed her as a training

center for 2,000 young cadets at a base at Rosyth, also in Scotland. She was traded, the Admiralty giving 24 old warships to the scrappers. The former *Majestic* was refitted and commissioned as the H.M.S. *Caledonia*, then (and rather oddly) the Royal Navy's largest ship in active service.

When war started in September 1939, the cadets were hurriedly removed from the *Caledonia* for fear of an air attack. While there was some talk of reactivating the ship as a troop transport, her powerless presence (her engines had been removed) was also considered a potential threat. She was shifted away from the main shipping channel in the Firth of Forth and deliberately beached. On September 29, she caught fire and burned beyond repair. Her remains were sold to the same scrap firm that had bought her in 1936, but she was not fully dismantled until the summer of 1943. By then, of all the big express liners of the 1920s, only the *Aquitania* was still in service. The *Mauretania*, the *Olympic* and the *Homeric* were gone, and the last skeletal remains of the *Berengaria* were nearby. They were finished off just after the war's end, in 1946. An era in transatlantic shipping—the age of the floating palaces, of the three-ship express runs and of the great heyday of the White Star Line—was over.

THE QUEENS:
THE MARY AND
THE ELIZABETH

TWO OF THE THREE greatest ocean liners ever built were the *Queen Mary* and her slightly larger companion ship, the *Queen Elizabeth* (the third of this great trio was the *Normandie* of the French Line). These were the only three ships in the 80,000-ton class. The story of the rivalry of the *Queen Mary* and the slightly younger *Normandie* would in itself make a book. Both claimed to be the world's largest liner, and both were—the Cunarder for only a very brief period. Both claimed to be the world's fastest and, again, both were—each in turn, although finally the *Queen Mary* won on this count. Standing alone was the *Queen Elizabeth*, from her first moments of active life to the very end the world's largest passenger ship. None has yet been built larger. However, new cruise ships in the planning stages will be two, three and even four times as large as the *Queen Elizabeth*. History has not been kind to her and, with the sad ending that befell her in the harbor of Hong Kong, the curtain fell on one of the truly great superships of our age, or of all time.

The *Queen Mary* was to have been named the *Victoria*, with the traditional -ia ending of nearly all Cunard steamships. When the time came to inform King George V of this decision, Sir Percy Bates and Sir Ashley Sparkes, two of the top people at Cunard, requested an audience at Buckingham Palace. It was left to Sir Ashley, who was Cunard's top representative in North America, to speak to the king. He said: "Your Majesty, we are pleased to inform you that Cunard wishes your approval to name our newest and greatest liner after England's greatest queen." Without a moment's hesitation, the king replied: "My wife would be delighted." And that was that. This account was told to Frank Braynard in 1946 by Vincent Demo, a Cunard executive who became cochairman of Cunard in North America. Frank Braynard told the story in his first book, published in 1947 as *Lives of the Liners*. For the next 42 years he was criticized for publicizing an "apocryphal" anecdote. Then in 1988, while attending a dinner party on Long Island, he was given the privilege of sitting at table with the grande dame of the area. She was thinking hard about how to open the conversation, and when she began, she startled Frank Braynard with her opening comment: "My favorite ship story," she said, smiling, "is about when my father went to see King George V." She was Eleanor Sparkes, and told the identical anecdote, almost word for word as Vincent Demo had related it 42 years earlier!

QUEEN MARY.

It is November 5, 1935, and work on the *Queen Mary* has progressed so rapidly that her maiden voyage has been set for May 1936. Interior decorators are aboard in droves and "have taken command of the ship" according to the caption pasted on the back of this striking photo released by *Planet News*, London. The ship's new gravity davits were also mentioned in the caption. A vast improvement over old-style davits, they permitted gravity to assist in the launching of the lifeboats. The especially wide extension of the bridge, with its little square wind-protection house, was a distinguishing feature. The old-style well deck forward of the superstructure was something few great liners had had for decades—a throwback that astonished ship historians. The *Queen Mary* was a combination of highly traditional styles and much that was ultramodern. She became one of the most successful liners in all history, a tribute to Cunard thinking and

knowledge of the marketplace. The *Normandie*, on the other hand, far ahead in hull design, revolutionary new interior techniques and decorative thinking, with vastly larger unencumbered deck space, failed to attract anything like as many passengers as did the Cunard flagship. No one seems to know why. It is possible that sailing on the French Line beauty was something like living in a cathedral—but that is just not enough of a reason. Someday someone will write a well-documented and thought-out study on the ships' brief period as competitors strictly from a salesman's standpoint. Just what did the *Queen Mary* have that was apparently lacking in the *Normandie*? [Built by John Brown & Company Limited, Clydebank, Scotland, 1936. 81,235 gross tons; 1,018 feet long; 118 feet wide; 39-foot draft. Steam turbines, quadruple screw. Service speed 28.5 knots. 2,139 passengers (776 first class, 784 tourist class, 579 third class).]

The Queen Mary. After her christening and launch, the *Queen Mary* sits at the fitting-out berth *(above)*. Her three stacks, the second and third shorter than the first, are in place. The entire hull is white; as yet, no lifeboats are fixed, but the entire outline, admired around the world, can be seen. The launching was made difficult by the narrowness of the River Clyde—in fact, despite massive precautions, the *Queen Mary* ran aground on the other side. This Wide World photograph was taken on January 17, 1936. Its caption noted that "the *Queen Mary* will leave Clydebank for Southampton in March, and will begin her maiden voyage from there on May 27th." At this point, her 81,000 gross tons made her, briefly, the world's largest liner. The French Line's new queen—the *Normandie*—had come out the year before with a gross of 79,000 tons. But she was in a shipyard being strengthened to reduce vibration problems and would shortly come out with a new tonnage of slightly over 83,000 tons! The British were horrified, but their sense of decorum would not permit them any more than a few verbal protests, to which the French replied that their ship had been remeasured twice and that one new measurement showed her to be of over 86,000 gross tons—would Cunard prefer that

they use that figure? A battle of the titans . . . and, for the moment, the French had won.

In a moment of tension, even peril, during the passage down the tortuous channel of the River Clyde to sea *(opposite)*, the *Queen Mary*, bound for Southampton on March 24, 1936, is just swinging toward the south bank and running aground. Many thousands are watching, holding their breath, for they know the dangers of the river. She has just left her fitting-out berth. The cranes of John Brown's great shipyard, home of so many Cunarders before her, can be clearly seen. Two tugs pull at the bow, and the swirl of the waters at her stern shows how she tried to avoid the dangers of the narrow channel. A sudden gust of wind had been the culprit, pushing against the 1,000-foot hull of the new Cunard flagship. Her bulk acted just like a giant sail, and her stern was swept out of control of the guiding tugs and onto the muddy bank of the south side. After an anxious half hour, she broke clear and continued on her way. The great square air funnels were a much-talked-about feature, as was the archaic well deck forward. But *Planet News* proudly called her "the greatest ship ever built," and there was none on hand in the crowd to say them nay.

THE *MARY'S* MAIDEN VOYAGE.

Three views show the welcome given the *Queen Mary* on her arrival at New York on June 1, 1936. A smoke-and-steam-laden view *(above)* tells us that winds from Jersey City were blowing smoke over toward Manhattan. The great new superliner, flag-bedecked, is slowly making her regal way up the Hudson. This was the day of the Hudson River Day Line and the Hudson River Night Line, not to mention a whole fleet of excursion boats, and representatives of all of them were on hand, carrying thousands of excited, cheering well-wishers. The four-deck excursion boat (just left of the Moran tug with the traditional white "M" on its tall smokestack) lists almost dangerously to starboard. To the far right two sprays of water are pumped into the air by a fireboat as a salute. Three airplanes circle the happy scene. White columns of "smoke" indicate that steam whistles were blowing their salutes. A man, probably a reporter, stands next to the flag on top of the pilothouse of the small craft at the lower-right

corner. All was excitement and high spirits, despite the fact that the new *Queen Mary* had failed to beat the *Normandie* and win the Blue Ribbon of the Atlantic. Her speed for the passage was four days, 12 hours and 20 minutes. The *Normandie* had done it in 38 fewer minutes the year before.

The lovely new liner passes West 42 Street on the hazy, overcast day *(opposite, top)*. A Black Diamond Line "Hog Islander" can be seen at the Weehawken pier. Above the *Mary's* stern is a two-stacked Hamburg-America Line steamer.

The great ship comes slowly into Pier 90 to end her maiden voyage *(opposite, bottom)*. Crowds pack the street, pier and buildings. The *Queen Mary* was the first superliner to use Pier 90, a new 1,100-foot-long structure specially built for Cunard's two new superliners. This unique view was captured by a photographer perched on the ship's mainmast. The three funnels are before him and the ship herself is being positioned into the north side of the pier.

Maintaining the Mary. Maintenance of all liners—and the Cunarders were certainly no exception—was a full-time task. The painting of the exterior, for example *(above, left)* required a specialist crew of painters and more paint than an entire small community would use. This scene, dating from the *Queen Mary*'s first full winter overhaul in February 1937, was referred to as the ship's first "beauty treatment." Thirty years later, in 1967, when the ship was retired from Cunard service, layers of paint over six inches thick would be on parts of her hull and superstructure.

A night photograph was taken while the *Queen Mary* was at the King George V Graving Dock at Southampton, where her hull was being scraped and painted *(above, right)*. Her gigantic bulk is thrown into relief by the powerful floodlights used to enable work to go on by night as well as by day. Her perfectly rounded cruiser stern and docking bridge are highlighted in this fine view, as are her four screws.

The *Mary*'s Interiors. The first-class lounge on the *Queen Mary* was a room in the grand tradition established by the two-deck-high public rooms on the *Imperator*, the *Vaterland* and the *Bismarck*. It was modern in some respects, but not too modern, elegant but not gaudy, vast but with cozy corners and three fireplaces around which easy chairs could be clustered for small gatherings of friends. The giant deck-to-ceiling carving on white dominated the room. The great frosted-glass light fixtures threw illumination upward in an early form of indirect lighting. The world is fortunate indeed that this wonderful ship is being preserved at Long Beach, California.

The *Mary*'s Interiors. Two views of the great first-class dining room on the *Queen Mary*: The first *(right, top)*, shows the room before the installation of its furniture. The huge wall map was used to track the daily position of the *Queen Mary* throughout the transatlantic voyage. Only on the Italian Line's superliner *Conte di Savoia* was another chart of such huge dimensions ever mounted. This one was especially brilliant in its design and feeling. The room is shown completed *right, bottom.*

A photograph taken March 11, 1936 *(opposite, top)*, shows workmen putting finishing touches to what is described by Wide World as "the motion picture theatre" on the new *Queen Mary*. It "will also be used as the ballroom," stated the caption on the back. Because of its flat deck, the room was not at all suited for motion pictures, and probably little used as a theater. Eventually Cunard created a space used exclusively for movies on the promenade deck, starboard side. It, too, was never really adequate because there was no rake to the floor—but it served. The completed main lounge is shown opposite, bottom.

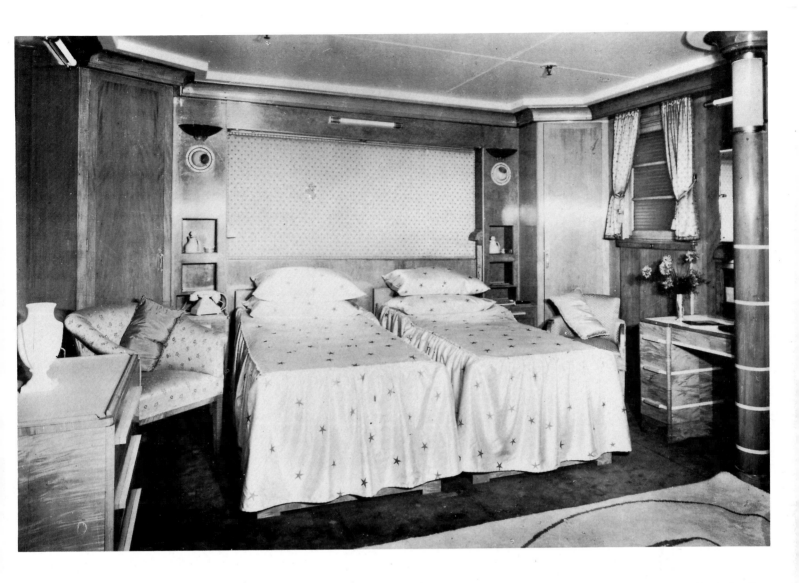

The *Mary*'s First-Class Accommodations. Far forward is the observation lounge and cocktail bar *(opposite, top)*, still much frequented on the ship in her permanent berth at Long Beach. Some friends of the ship have been a bit shaken to find soda being sold here, but there are many who might even say this was an improvement. A rarer view *(opposite, bottom)* shows the *Mary*'s small and exclusive Verandah Grill, with the main mast rising in its center, blocking a full view of the striking mural on the forward bulkhead.

In a first-class stateroom *(above)*, handsome polished woodwork gives a feeling of warmth, augmenting good solid comfort and plenty of elbow room. Two modest-sized American vessels forced Cunard and most other transatlantic carriers to abandon the "first-class" category in the Depression. They were the *Manhattan* and the *Washington*, 30,000-gross-ton sisters built at the New York Shipbuilding Corporation yard at Camden, New Jersey. They were so called "cabin-class" ships, offering top-category space at considerably less than the first-class rates. All was done according to rules set up by the august Transatlantic Passenger Conference of Brussels. This gave these United States Lines ships such an advantage, as their owners had hoped it would, that the other major lines all adopted the cabin, tourist and tourist-third classification on their ships.

QUEEN ELIZABETH.

On her first voyage, the newly launched *Queen Elizabeth (opposite)*, in the care of River Clyde tugboats, is repositioned at the fitting-out dock at the John Brown shipyards after launching. Already a 40,000-ton ship, on September 27, 1938, she had just been christened, in the presence of nearly half a million guests and spectators, by Queen Elizabeth (the present Queen Mother). King George VI was also expected to attend but, because of the increasingly worrisome situation with the Germans, had to cancel. The Queen was accompanied by her two daughters, Princess Elizabeth and Princess Margaret. In a little less than 30 years, in September 1967, Princess Elizabeth, as queen, would return to the same Clydebank shipyard to christen the successor ocean sovereign, the *Queen Elizabeth 2*.

Winston Churchill ordered the *Queen Elizabeth* to be brought to New York for safety from air attack. The trickle of white steam from the three-throated whistle on her forward stack indicates that the great new ship is saluting as she approaches New York's Lower Bay and the Hudson River on her secret maiden voyage *(above)*. It is March 7, 1940, and words of the surprise arrival of the world's largest passenger ship causes great excitement in maritime circles. A Coast Guard cutter is leading her in. The ship's clean-cut bridge face is distinctive, as is the fact that she has two huge funnels, not three. There is no well deck. In this view one cannot see the degaussing cables running along her main deck to protect her from magnetic mines. Unlike the *Queen Mary*, she has a bow anchor. She was not in port long. After a quick conversion to trooping service, she was off to join the *Queen Mary* in six years of war use. [Built by John Brown & Company Limited, Clydebank, Scotland, 1940. 83,673 gross tons; 1,031 feet long; 118 feet wide; 39-foot draft. Steam turbines, quadruple screw. Service speed 28.5 knots. 2,283 passengers (823 first class, 662 cabin class, 798 tourist class).]

NEW YORK, MARCH 7, 1940.
A classic and extremely rare photograph captures the three largest liners in the world side by side. They are (left to right): the *Normandie* at Pier 88, north side; the *Queen Mary* at Pier 90, south side and the *Queen Elizabeth* arriving at the north side of Pier 90. The *Queen Elizabeth*'s master, Captain J. C. Townley, said that the trip over was "just like a lovely cruise." The *Associated Press* described the *Elizabeth*'s crossing as a "dramatic six-day zigzag." It added: "The three ships will remain in New York for the duration of the war." Behind the *Normandie*, in gray camouflage paint, is Cunard's new *Mauretania*, built in 1939. She was already in "heavy" war use at that point, as the two Queens would shortly be.

THE QUEENS DURING WAR.

The *Queen Elizabeth (above)* leaves New York for war service in November 1940, the empty *Normandie* to the left. The massive service of the *Queen Mary* and the *Queen Elizabeth* in moving hundreds of thousands of men quickly all over the globe was one of the greatest achievements of maritime history during the war. The sale of the *Leviathan* for scrap, only months before bombs began to fall, and the burning of the *Normandie* at her New York pier in 1942 were two Allied disasters that, in the long run, had great impact on our cause. Had these two great liners, each capable of moving 15,000 troops at 26 knots or better, been available, the war might have been shortened by many months. It is interesting to note that someone neglected to remove or cover over the name *Queen Elizabeth*, still evident in the bow.

In the war years, both Queens were refitted to carry nearly eight times their peacetime capacities. Every conceivable space was used so that 8,000 service personnel could sleep at any given time while a second "sleep shift" could hold a further 8,000. Standee bunks were placed four-high in the *Queen Mary*'s forward observation lounge *(opposite, top)* and a suite was restyled for 18 officers *(opposite, bottom)*.

The Queens During War. A Navy blimp hovers over the *Queen Elizabeth* on one of her departures from New York *(opposite)*. Her name has been painted over. The degaussing cable is in place. Her upper deck is crowded with officers. They had more freedom to move around than ordinary G.I.s, who were usually kept far below. Perhaps it is summertime, for under magnification the photograph shows some figures in summer whites. There was only one crow's nest on the *Queen Elizabeth*, and she has temporary coverings at the outer ends of the bridge.

At the end of the war, the two Queens remained under military control to return troops. The *Queen Mary (above, top)* receives a noisy welcome as she prepares to tie up at her old berth, the Ocean Dock, at Southampton, on August 11, 1945, for the first time in six years. The display of signal flags is the only evidence that peace has returned. She was not decommissioned until September 1946.

An updated photograph of the *Queen Elizabeth (above, bottom)*, shows her bringing troops home. A group of uniformed women—Wacs, Wrens and the like—wave greetings to the soldiers crowding the decks and upper works of the huge liner. The stem anchor is down and at the ready. The ship is decked out with signal pennants. The view shows how much sleeker the *Elizabeth* looked without the well deck forward, which designers of the *Queen Mary* put on her as a bow to the distant past of ship design.

RETURN TO PEACE.

By October 1945, the British government had allowed Cunard to paint the stacks of the *Queen Elizabeth* in peacetime colors for the first time *(above)*. Because the stacks were so much thicker and longer, only two black dividing stripes were needed in the orange-red section. The stack, therefore, was divided into four equal parts— the black top and three wide orange-red sections. The photograph was taken by the Royal Canadian Air Force while the *Elizabeth* was being used to ferry Canadian troops home to Halifax, where she is seen being refueled.

The *Queen Elizabeth* was still under control of the military when, on March 8, 1946, a bad fire developed while she was at Southampton *(right)*. Police and Cunard–White Star staff probed its cause. It had broken out, so it was said, in the isolation hospital. The fire was extinguished after dockhands and firemen had fought it for one and a half hours. On June 16, the ship was handed back to her owners for restoration.

MODELS OF THE QUEENS.

A 22-foot-long model of the *Queen Mary (above, top)* is having its finishing touches done at the Bassett-Lowke, Ltd., model shop in Northampton, England. It was made for Cunard to be displayed at its American headquarters. The company moved and, in 1971, it was given as a gift to Frank Braynard for the South Street Seaport Museum. The Seaport eventually loaned it on a long-term basis to the *Queen Mary* in Long Beach, where it has remained on display.

Many hands help as a 22-foot-long scale model of the *Queen Elizabeth (above, bottom)* is carefully moved into 25 Broadway, Cunard's main office in the United States, where it went on display in the huge four-story-high domed booking hall. Also built by Bassett-

Lowke, Ltd., it was part of one of the greatest exhibits of ship models displayed by any single company. There was also a wonderful 16-foot-long model of the *Majestic*, later given to South Street Seaport Museum. Stolen one night, it has never been recovered. A similar model is now in the Science Museum at Toronto. Also on display at 25 Broadway was a superb model of the *Mauretania* of 1907. The late Ralph E. Cropley, maritime historian and curator of the Seamen's Church Institute of New York's fine maritime museum at 25 South Street, believed that it had originally been a *Lusitania* model, carefully disguised. Another great model was that of the *Berengaria*. There were also smaller models of the *Media*, the *Alsatia* and the *Britannia* and other early Cunard paddle steamers.

THE POSTWAR ERA:
THE FINAL ATLANTIC FLEET

MORE THAN ANY OTHER steamship firm's, Cunard's fleet taught us what beautiful ships should look like, with their charcoal-black hulls, raked bows and curved sterns, snow-white upperworks, neatly nested rows of lifeboats and, of course, those extraordinary stacks—one, two or three of them in that glowing orange-red and offset by black tops and the narrow stripes. They were all visions that made memorable impressions.

"Getting there is half the fun" was not only a slogan of marketing genius, but it was absolutely true as well. Cunard offered some of the very best, most frequent and diverse transatlantic services in the years after the Second World War. In the 1950s, that last buoyant decade before the dramatic, all-changing arrival of the jet, Cunard proudly reported that it carried a third of all passengers on the Atlantic route. In 1955 alone, there were over 300 different sailings from North American ports.

In the summer of 1947, the old "express run" between New York, Cherbourg and Southampton was at its best and the renewal of the Queens created the first two-ship relay. There was a sailing every Wednesday from New York and every Thursday from Southampton, and then, somewhere in mid-North Atlantic, the "royal pair" would pass one another at a combined speed of nearly 60 knots! The splendid second *Mauretania* assisted in peak times.

The *Mauretania*'s companion might have been the 34,000-tonner ordered in 1946. But, in looking over the 1930s in particular, Cunard keenly realized that there was a future—in fact, a big future—in cruising. And so, the *Caronia* was finished as a large, green-colored "yacht," a floating country club with 600 cruise passengers being looked after by 600 handpicked staff on long, expensive cruises. She became one of the most important ships of her time and has left a legendary reputation.

In those immediate postwar years, Cunard also added two ships unusual for the company—a pair intended as freighters that were redesigned as combination passenger–cargo liners with 250 berths each, all of them in first class. Katharine Hepburn once remarked that the *Media* and her twin ship, the *Parthia*, were her favorite Atlantic ships.

There were also remnants of the prewar fleet. The grand old *Aquitania* was back, at least for a few years, but only in austerity service and often with more troops and war brides and refugees than actual cabin passengers. Four of the single-stackers from the twenties returned as well: the *Scythia*, the *Samaria*, the *Franconia* and the *Ascania*. Finally, one member of the old White Star fleet was restored luxuriously. She was the *Britannic* and she kept her original funnel colors to the end, in 1960, even if the Cunard–White Star name had been dropped a decade before. The prewar *Georgic* also reappeared, although demoded to budget service for about a half-dozen summers. There was even a special charter: In 1950, one of P&O's big Australian liners, the *Stratheden*, made four trips across to New York to help with the overflow of travelers.

Cunard's only new tonnage in the 1950s was a quartet for the Canadian run—the *Saxonia*, the *Ivernia*, the *Carinthia* and the *Sylvania*. But the tide was turning. Just as the *Sylvania* made her debut in 1957, the airlines reported carrying as many passengers as the steamer companies. The jet made its first appearance in the following year. The writing was on the wall.

The 1960s were almost ruinous for Cunard. The staunch, conservative directors at Liverpool, in their great marble-clad boardroom and offices that themselves echoed of yesterday, would not concede. They insisted that the general public would always prefer the likes of the grand old *Queen Mary* to a speedy new 707. They were wrong. By 1965, the airlines could not have been more successful, carrying nearly 95 percent of all Atlantic passengers.

At first, Cunard's token gesture to the future, to this big change, was to redo the *Saxonia* and the *Ivernia* as part-time cruise ships. But the miscalculations persisted: attempting to open a "new" Mediterranean service, but with the aged *Mauretania;* giving the *Queen Elizabeth* a costly refit as though air-conditioning and plastic flowers in the lounge could really make her an adequate tropical cruise ship; the continuance of traditional midwinter crossings (the *Elizabeth* once steamed into New York with 200 passengers served by 1,100 crew!). There was even serious talk of a three-class liner, a design already outmoded, to replace the veteran *Queen Mary.*

Finally, the company faced harsh reality in the spring of 1966, when word was flashed that the Queens and almost all other Cunarders were to be retired. The curtain was coming down quickly. In prompt succession, the *Queen Mary*, the *Caronia*, the *Carinthia*, the *Sylvania* and the *Queen Elizabeth* left the active lists; only the restyled *Carmania* (ex-*Saxonia*) and the *Franconia* (ex-*Ivernia*) remained. Then, of course, there was the "big gamble," as newspapers called her—the 65,000-tonner that was started in 1965. She would be the center-piece of Cunard's future as part-time Atlantic liner, part-time cruise ship. She would be the third Queen, the *Queen Elizabeth 2.*

There is a poignant story about the final months of the *Queen Elizabeth*, in 1968. Costly maintenance had been greatly reduced, so her once-immaculate superstructure and hull were streaked with orange rust. Queen Elizabeth the Queen Mother, hearing that the ship she had christened in 1938 was soon to be decommissioned, requested a visit. Cunard was honored, but also mortified—what about the rust! In the end, only one side of the ship, the side that the Queen Mother would see, was freshly painted. Some years later, in 1984, while addressing the Southampton branch of the World Ship Society, Bill Miller told this tale. A retired Cunard officer was in the audience. At the end of the talk, he rose and added: "That was an interesting story about the paint, but incorrect! In those difficult times, we painted only one side on *all* of our liners—the sides that the passengers would see!"

NEW YORK, 1956.

The Cunarders had always been familiar visitors to the Port of New York. In the fifties, there were often two and sometimes even as many as three or four arrivals and departures each week. In a helicopter view taken from 800 feet in midafternoon on September 17, 1956, the *Queen Mary* is inbound, steaming upriver and soon to land nearly 2,000 passengers, their baggage and some priority cargo. Hoboken is in the foreground. On the far left is an Anchor Line freighter and then one from the Holland-America Line. The three piers in the center have just opened for the American Export Lines. At the right is the Lackawanna Railroad ferry terminal. In mid-river, near the big Cunarder, is a Gulf Oil Company tanker and a New York Central Railroad ferry. The busy Manhattan piers behind range from Pier 61, at West 21 Street, on the left, down to Pier 45, West 10 Street, on the right.

DOCKING AT NEW YORK.

The *Queen Mary* arrives at New York *(opposite, top)*. Apart from the *Normandie*, the Queens were the largest liners that ever used the Port of New York. Until 1963, they berthed at Pier 90, on the north slip, an 1,100-foot-long terminal that had to be dredged constantly for them. Because of their extraordinary draft of 39 feet, both of the big Cunarders often had to move with the ever-changing tides. Consequently, in the nearly yearlong weekly tandems, the *Queen Mary* might arrive on a Tuesday morning at 8 and sail the following day at 11:30. On the following week, the *Queen Elizabeth* might arrive, again on a Tuesday, but at 2 in the afternoon and then sail at 6 on Wednesday evening. The schedule was constantly changing and

sometimes even included a midnight sailing and at least one winter Saturday morning departure at 9:30.

Five or six tugs were used to berth the mighty Queens. In a view of October 1949 *(opposite, bottom)* the *Mary* is being maneuvered off Pier 90 by five Moran tugs, three pushing on the starboard bow and two at work on the port stern.

It was sometimes a very tight squeeze at New York. While slips between Cunard Piers 90 and 92 stretched for two city blocks, the shifts and turns necessitated very careful handling. On October 30, 1956, the *Mary (above)* is being gently nudged by three tugs into the north slip of Pier 90 while the *Britannic* is already at berth on the south side of Pier 92.

Docking at New York. Safe and secure, the *Queen Mary* is now moored alongside Pier 90. Her passengers are in the lounges, foyers and along the enclosed promenades, awaiting calls for customs and immigration, and then for disembarkation. In this view of 1948, nine Moran tugs are involved in the docking process. The small American cruise ship *Borinquen* is at the left, berthed on the south side of Pier 92, and the French Line's *De Grasse* is just above the big Cunarder, at the north side of Pier 88.

Docking at New York. While a normal, tug-assisted docking at New York took about 35 minutes, there were tense occasions when, with the tugs on strike, ships such as the mighty Queens had to berth themselves. Using their own power for each step and being guided by a small boat (often one of the ship's own lifeboats), the process took well over two hours. With the captain and his other senior officers busy on the bridge, Cunard officials nervously watched from shore. On only one occasion was there any mishap. When the *Queen Elizabeth*, attempting to turn into the slip between Piers 90 and 92, was pushed by a fierce wind, the uppermost portion of her bow bent the catwalk on the rooftop cargo-handling rigs.

PROVISIONING AND CARGO (*opposite*).
Unloading, loading and provisioning were designed to be efficiently, systematically and, above all, quickly done. At New York, the ships were rarely at dock longer than 24 hours—2,000 or so passengers and their luggage off on Tuesday; 2,000 new passengers aboard on Wednesday. In the interim, there were general housecleaning and inventory for 31,000 sheets and an equal number of pillowcases, 21,000 tablecloths, 92,000 linen napkins, 2,400 bath mats, 2,200 afternoon tea cloths, 4,100 blankets and a supply of 7,900 aprons for the various kitchen departments. Provisioning the giant freezers and vast storerooms for a five-day crossing meant 20 tons of meat, 4,000 chickens and ducklings, 20 tons of fish, 70,000 eggs, 4,000 pounds of tea and coffee, 30 tons of potatoes, 10,000 bottles of wine, 60,000 bottles of mineral water, 40,000 pounds of vegetables, 4,000 gallons of milk, three tons of butter, 10,000 pounds of sugar, 600 crates of apples and oranges, 2,000 pounds of cheese and 40,000 bottles of beer. In the kitchens, there were over 800 saucepans, and one electric stove measured 16 feet in length. A breakfast menu could include 20 kinds of cereal, 18 kinds of bread and rolls and 15 different jams and marmalades. Cunard publicity material often mentioned that there

were eight different kinds of bacon for breakfast. In a view of October 24, 1946 (*opposite, top*), two Esso tugs are maneuvering an oil barge to the port side of the mighty *Queen Elizabeth*. Within seven hours, she will take on 7,000 tons of bunker fuel.

All of the big Cunard liners carried some cargo—baggage and such priority items as gold bullion, mail and diplomatic items. There were also antique cars, artworks and Irish racehorses aboard the *Britannic*. In a view of February 4, 1948 (*opposite, bottom*), baggage is being unloaded from the *Queen Mary* at New York.

LUXURY LINER ROW, 1958 (*above*).
Until the 1960s, the world's greatest and grandest ocean liners could often be seen berthed at New York, along the West Side, between West 44 and West 57 Streets, in Luxury Liner Row. Cunarders were almost always represented. This view of July 9, 1958 captured the largest gathering at New York since the end of the Second World War. Three Cunarders are present: the *Britannic* (barely visible at the bottom); the giant *Queen Elizabeth* and the *Mauretania*. Beyond are the *Liberté*, the *United States*, the *America*, the *Constitution* and the *Vulcania*.

THE RISING TIDE.

One of Cunard's finest postwar advertising booklets was one titled *The Rising Tide.* A quote from one section seems appropriate to this trio of photographs, all made by Everett Viez when he was crossing on the *Queen Mary* in October 1956:

> The last of the ship's visitors, returning to shore, look back, not without envy. The ship's bands play. The ship's engines whisper. Soon the land starts to slide away from the liner. On shore, the diminishing figures in the whirl you left behind you, walk faster and faster, waving excitedly, along the pier.
>
> The *Queen* goes preening down the water, as pretty as paint, as serene as a Rolls-Royce, and as sure as the Bank of England. Now, the liberated passenger takes a deep breath and starts to realize that he has just crossed the frontier into another world. A world where

no one from the world ashore can get at him, unless he wants them to; but where he can get any of the shore-people, simply by lifting the telephone in his cabin.

He has entered a world, moreover, where space is everyone's heritage, and time is of little account. As the new passenger starts to explore the ship, with something of the same sort of wonder and excitement as he might explore the city of Venice, there is one apocalyptic notice that catches his eye. On the eastward voyage, the notice says, "Clocks will be put forward 20 minutes at 5 P.M., 20 minutes at 11 P.M. and 20 minutes at 2 A.M." Which adds up to a 23-hour day. And on the westward voyage the notice says: "Clocks will stop for an hour at midnight." Which adds up to a 25-hour day. Time stands still, and it doesn't matter. To the busy executive, whose hectic life on land has been tyrannized by clocks, it makes a pleasant change to find that the clock, for once, is his servant and not his master. Clocks will stop for one hour at midnight. Travelling in this timeless way, by sea—what is an hour one way or another?

NOTABLE PASSENGERS.
International celebrities were often aboard the Cunarders, usually the Queens. In these scenes from the 1950s, actors Charles Boyer and Spencer Tracy chat on the enclosed promenade *(right, top);* actress Madeleine Carroll and her husband pause on deck *(right, middle)* and Sir Winston and Lady Churchill arrive in the main lounge of the *Queen Mary* for a party *(right, bottom).*

OCEAN TERMINAL.

The famed boat trains relayed passengers between Southampton's Ocean Terminal and London's Waterloo Station. As many as a dozen railway coaches carried passengers, with fares that were $4 in first class in the late fifties (they had climbed to nearly $40 by the late 1980s) and $2 in second class. Some passengers even took entire compartments for the two-hour ride. This aerial view, taken in the early fifties, shows the *Queen Elizabeth* to the left. She has just

departed from the Ocean Terminal, a late Art Deco structure completed in 1950 and demolished in 1983, when the site became a scrap-metal depot. The terminal, partially obscured in this view, is just to the right of center and to the right of the two white-hulled British troopships at dock. The *Queen Elizabeth 2* uses the Queen Elizabeth II Terminal, which was completed in the late 1960s along the same dockhead.

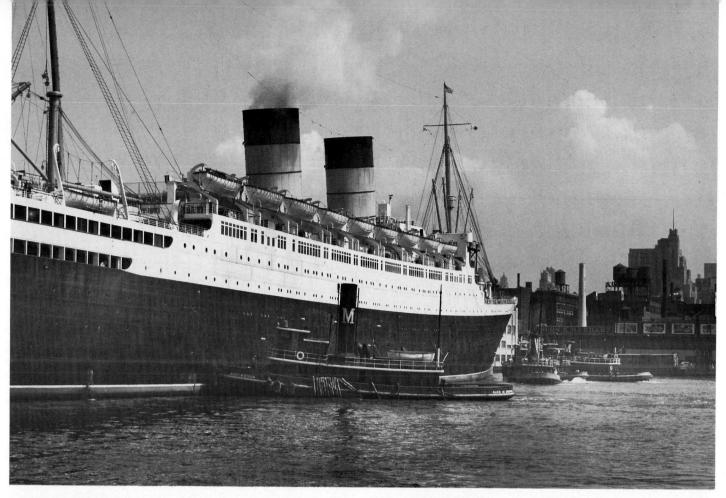

THE SECOND *MAURETANIA*.

At the *Mauretania*'s launching in July 1938, Lady Bates, the wife of the Cunard chairman, did the honors and remarked: "I count myself extremely fortunate in having been asked to launch this great ship. This is a red-letter day, not only for me but for Merseyside. The launch of the largest ship ever built in England, I hope that like her namesake she may work her way into the affections of all who have anything to do with her on both sides of the Atlantic." The new *Mauretania* had barely entered commercial service when the Second World War started. She was quickly painted in gray and sailed for the next seven years as a trooper. She went back to Cunard service in April 1947, as the "relief ship," when needed, on the Southampton–New York express run. Otherwise, she maintained much of a more relaxed, independent service—sailing every three weeks or so between Southampton, Le Havre, Cobh and New York. She had a loyal following in her own right, but the triumphs of her predecessor, that glorious four-stacker that had held the Blue Ribbon for 22 years, always stole her thunder. Otherwise, this ship's rather arcane distinction of being the largest liner yet built in England (bigger British ships having been built in either Scotland or Northern

Ireland) held until 1960, with the advent of the new *Windsor Castle* and *Oriana*.

Unlike the two Queens, the *Mauretania* went cruising in the winter, off-season period—usually on two- and three-week Caribbean cruises from New York.

The *Mauretania*, which had her debut between the delivery of the *Queen Mary* and that of the *Queen Elizabeth*, was actually more like the latter. She was often said to be the *Elizabeth*'s "first cousin." Both had two-funnel exteriors, and similar interiors. Both were done in a late Art Deco style—lighter, softer and perhaps less grand than the *Queen Mary*. There was a coziness about them.

These views show the *Mauretania*'s lounge in first class (called cabin class when she was completed in 1939, *above, left*); the first-class restaurant *(above, right)* and the tourist-class lounge (which was third class before the war; *below*). [Built by Cammell Laird & Company, Birkenhead, England, 1939. 35,655 gross tons; 772 feet long; 89 feet wide; 30-foot draft. Steam turbines, twin screw. Service speed 23 knots. 1,140 passengers (470 first class, 370 cabin class, 300 tourist class).]

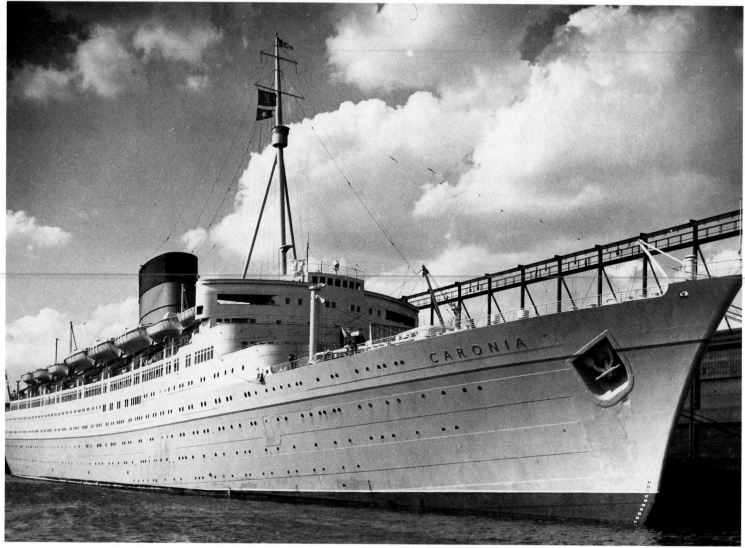

western Mediterranean—to Gibraltar, Naples, Genoa and Cannes—a misguided venture at best. But how could she ever hope to compete, not only on a route where the Cunard name was virtually unknown, but against such flashier, better-fitted types as the *Leonardo da Vinci* and the *Cristoforo Colombo* of the Italian Line? The *Mauretania* went back promptly to periodic Southampton service, but mostly cruises. At the end, there was even a charter to carry guests to the opening of a new refinery. She was decommissioned in November 1965 and, after a few cherished items were removed at Southampton, she sailed northward to Inverkeithing in Scotland and the local scrappers. The name is still well remembered. In 1983, when Cunard bought Norway's *Vistafjord* and *Sagafjord*, two deluxe cruise ships, it was for a time considered renaming one of them the *Mauretania*.

CARONIA (*opposite, bottom*).

The *Caronia* was a distinguished ship. When completed at the end of 1948, she was the largest liner to have only one funnel (and that funnel was one of the biggest ever to go to sea). She had the tallest mast afloat. She was certainly the largest liner ever to be painted entirely in green—four different shades in all, giving her the nickname of "the Green Goddess." In Cunard annals, she was the first liner to have a built-in outdoor pool and the first to have private toilets and either bath or shower in all of her staterooms, regardless of class. Most important, she was the largest liner yet built to cruise almost year-round. It was a daring and successful venture. She was the great forerunner to the cruise fleets that would come two decades later.

In 1945–46, it was thought that the *Caronia* would be used on the transatlantic run as a companion to the *Mauretania*, and would cruise only periodically. But this plan was revised completely by the earliest stages of construction at the John Brown yards. Her interiors were reduced versions of those on the *Queen Elizabeth*, built at the same shipyard.

A very grand cruise ship, the *Caronia* was designed for a reduced capacity of 600 passengers, most of them elderly and wealthy. They were attended by an equal number of crew. In fact, the ship often carried as few as 300, making her the "millionaires' yacht" and the "world's largest floating country club." Some devoted passengers lived aboard for months, some for years, and one woman, creating an unsurpassed record, sailed continuously for nearly 15 years, giving Cunard an estimated $4 million in fares.

The *Caronia*'s patterns were prescribed: in January, a cruise of just over three months around the world, up and down the Pacific or around Africa; in spring, it was six to eight weeks in the Mediterranean; in summer, six weeks in Scandinavia; and finally, in fall, six to eight weeks in the Mediterranean. There was the occasional transatlantic crossing for positioning and sometimes a two-week end-of-summer cruise to the West Indies.

The *Caronia* had a definite clubbiness about her. Her decor was in British ocean-liner style: polished woods and chrome lighting fixtures, etched mirrors, lino floors and overstuffed chairs and sofas. Everthing about her was crisp and precise. She was often said to be the most luxurious ship in the world, some people claiming that she even surpassed first class in the two Queens. There were handpicked stewards in impeccably starched whites, teas at four and lots of cooking to order at dinnertime. Returning from their excursions on shore, passengers often found their favorite drinks ready, the dinner clothes laid out and a warm bath drawn. It was all like a grand old seaside hotel. There was a sense of the familiar; many of her passengers, having been aboard before, knew one another and knew what to expect. Often they insisted on the same stateroom year after year.

The main lounge (*left, top*) is dominated by a portrait of Princess (now Queen) Elizabeth and Prince Philip. In appreciation of Cunard's wartime service, and since the *Caronia* was the largest liner yet built in postwar Britain, the Princess had christened the ship in October 1947. The ship had two restaurants that were named after royal residences, Balmoral and Sandringham (*left, middle*). Cabin A-41 (*left, bottom*), was typical for Cunard at the time—the wood furniture, the wardrobes, the beds with their satin spreads. The *Caronia* had forced-air ventilation until the mid-fifties when, like several other Cunarders, she was given full air-conditioning. [Built by John Brown & Company Limited, Clydebank, Scotland, 1948. 34,172 gross tons; 715 feet long; 91 feet wide; 31-foot draft. Steam turbines, twin screw. Service speed 22 knots. 932 passengers (581 first class, 351 cabin class); 600 passengers for all-first-class cruising.]

The Mauretania (*opposite, top*). The *Mauretania* was quick to fall on hard times after the first onslaught of the jet. By the early sixties, on the traditional Southampton run, she was often carrying as little as a third of her capacity. Cunard management sought desperate alternatives, not always with the best foresight. In 1962, the *Mauretania* was given a cosmetic makeover, as if to disguise an aging lady. She was painted entirely in green, no doubt to remind the public of leisurely cruising and of the green of the fabled *Caronia*, and less of the old, drearier Northern trades. A year later, she was even pressed into a new Cunard service of regular sailings between New York and the

MEDIA.

A Cunard affiliate, the Brocklebank Line, had two big freighters on order in 1945-46. Cunard, wanting to restore something of its prewar Liverpool–New York service, took the ships over and had them redesigned as combination passenger–cargo ships with 250 all-first-class passengers and six holds of cargo—unique vessels in the Cunard fleet. They became the *Media*, added in August 1947, and the *Parthia*, which first arrived in April 1948. The *Media* was, in fact, the first new Atlantic passenger ship to be completed after the war. Both became very popular, especially because of their comparatively intimate accommodations and their more relaxed eight-to-ten-day crossings. Their voyages sometimes included diversions, including calls at Norfolk in Virginia, at Bermuda and at Greenock in Scotland. Before labor charges at the New York City docks became prohibitively high, these ships tended to say in port for as long as six days, arriving on Saturday and sailing the following Friday. Sometimes, when Cunard's berths were crowded, they even had to be shifted across the Hudson to the Eighth Street pier in Hoboken. The *Media* and *Parthia*

were known to be "poor sea boats," but in 1952, Cunard tested the first fin stabilizers used on the often ferocious North Atlantic on the *Media*. It was a considerable success and soon such stabilizers went to all Cunarders and most other Atlantic liners.

In 1961, when jets grabbed most of the ships' clientele, and when their cargos began to go in faster, larger freighters, the *Media* and *Parthia* were sold. The *Media* became the Italian immigrant-transport *Flavia*, later a cruise liner, enduring until early 1989, when she was destroyed by fire at Hong Kong. The *Parthia* became the *Remuera* and then the *Aramac* for British owners, trading in the Pacific, until scrapped on Taiwan in 1970.

In a view taken in June 1960, the *Media* is at the far left, the *Caronia*, the *Queen Mary* and the *Britannic* are next in the Cunard piers. They are followed by the *Liberté*, the *America*, the *Saturnia* and the *Independence*. [Built by John Brown & Company Limited, Clydebank, Scotland, 1947. 13,345 gross tons; 531 feet long; 70 feet wide; 30-foot draft. Steam turbines, twin screw. Service speed 18 knots. 250 first-class passengers.]

GEORGIC (above).

From 1949 through 1955, the *Britannic*'s near-sister, the *Georgic*, was under charter to Cunard in peak summer service, providing a budget service for tourists, immigrants and other groups. She was, because of her extensive war damage, a demoted ship: One stack was gone, she was all-tourist class and, because of structural problems resulting from her wartime fire, she was not even allowed to sail the North Atlantic in winter. In the off seasons, she took British emigrants to Australia and New Zealand. In summer, the *Georgic* sailed on a monthly schedule between either Liverpool or Southampton, Le Havre, Cobh, Halifax (to land Canadian passengers) and finally New York. In this aerial view of May 28, 1952, she is seen on the far left, berthed on the south side of Pier 90 in New York. The *Queen Mary* is being undocked, and the *Mauretania* and the *Media* share Pier 92. In 1956, the *Georgic* went to Scottish breakers at Faslane.

BRITANNIC (left).

The *Britannic* was the only survivor of the prewar White Star Line fleet to be fully restored. Also marked by a certain clubbiness, she ran a popular monthly service between New York, Cobh and Liverpool. Her passenger figures had been reduced after the war from 1,553 to 993 (429 in first class and 564 in tourist). Although she was without air-conditioning and had no amenities such as an outdoor pool, the *Britannic* left New York each January on a nine-week Mediterranean cruise. Her itinerary for January 1960 included Madeira, Casablanca, Tangier, Malta, Alexandria, Haifa, Larnaca, Rhodes, Istanbul, the Dardanelles, Piraeus, Dubrovnik, Venice, Messina, Naples, Villefranche, Barcelona, Palma, Algiers, Malaga, Gibraltar, Lisbon, Cherbourg and Southampton. Minimum fares were set at $1,275 and all rates included first-class return to New York on any Cunarder taken within the following 12 months.

Although the Cunard–White Star name had been dropped by 1950, the *Britannic* retained the original White Star black-and-buff stacks to her end, in December 1960. Her final year, her thirtieth (about normal retirement age for most liners), was troubled by mechanical disabilities that kept her at her New York berth for much of her final summer season. Her repairs ranked as the most extensive done at an ordinary liner berth.

AQUITANIA, 1948.

The *Aquitania*, the last four-stacker and the last of the floating palaces of pre–World War I days, was also back in Cunard service in the late forties. In view of her age, however, she was not fully restored, instead working an austerity service between Southampton and Halifax. While she catered to a few regular passengers in those otherwise busy times, for the most part, she carried troops, war brides, children, emigrants and refugees. Many had no luggage whatsoever, and were beginning new lives in the Canadian interior. At 35, she made her last runs in 1949. These were not uneventful, for she was rotting almost everywhere. Some bulkheads were threadbare, the funnels nearly crumbled and a piano almost crashed to the deck below when a ceiling

gave way. In February 1950, she was delivered to ship breakers in Scotland, one of the most outstanding, beloved and successful big liners ever. She had served in two world wars, steamed three million miles and made nearly 450 voyages. Just as she ranked as the last four-stacker, Cunard also had the last three-stacker, the *Queen Mary*, retired in 1967.

In this view of Southampton's New Docks, dated December 16, 1948, the *Aquitania* is in the foreground, no doubt preparing for another voyage to Nova Scotia. Ahead of her are the *Washington*, the *Stirling Castle* and the *Queen Mary* and, then in the far distance, the *Queen Elizabeth*. A strike had just ended and so the three largest Cunarders were together in the same port at the same time.

IVERNIA *(above, top).*
Cunard built only four new passenger liners in the 1950s, the *Saxonia*, the *Ivernia*, the *Carinthia* and the *Sylvania*. Delivered between 1954 and 1957, they were actually large passenger–cargo ships (about 900 passengers and six holds of freight). They were created to replace all of the old prewar liners (the *Scythia*, the *Samaria*, the *Franconia* and the *Ascania*) on the St. Lawrence route to Quebec City and Montreal. The first two were used out of Southampton, Le Havre and Cobh; the second pair from Liverpool and Greenock. These ships also represented a new dimension for Cunard and a fast-growing trend in Atlantic passenger-ship design. There were only two classes: a small first class on the upper deck, with most of the rest of the ship given over to tourist class in quarters vastly superior to those of the past. It appeared, at least for a time, that while the first-class trade was defecting to the airlines, tourist-class travel still showed a promising future. In fact, it too was already declining.

The *Ivernia*, shown on the River Thames in February 1959, highlights the balance of design: passenger accommodations midships and cargo gear forward and aft. The overall design, again done by the John Brown yards at Clydebank, clearly reflects the *Caronia* of little more than five years before. There is the same single stack (modernized with a dome for better exhaust), the sole mast above the bridge and the graduated decks aft. [Built by John Brown & Company Limited, Clydebank, Scotland, 1955. 21,717 gross tons; 608 feet long; 80 feet wide. Steam turbines, twin screw. Service speed 19.5 knots. 925 passengers (125 first class, 800 tourist class).]

CARINTHIA *(above, bottom).*
The *Carinthia*, launched by Princess Margaret, is shown in one of F. Leonard Jackson's evocative views at another well-known Cunard terminal: the Prince's Landing Stage at Liverpool. Cunard's headquarters was a short distance away. But Cunard soon favored Southampton over Liverpool for its sailings even though, in the years before the First World War, Liverpool had been the "big ship" terminal to and from New York for such liners as the *Mauretania* and *Lusitania*. But in a time of almost constant change and of scrambling for better results prompted by worried accountants, the Cunard Liverpool services were finally eliminated and the *Carinthia* and her sister, the *Sylvania*, made the final company trips out of the historic port in 1966–67. Over 20 years later, in July 1990, the *QE2* called there for the first time as part of a weeklong celebratory cruise marking Cunard's hundred-fiftieth anniversary. [Built by John Brown & Company Limited, Clydebank, Scotland, 1956. 21,947 gross tons; 608 feet long; 80 feet wide. Steam turbines, twin screw. Service speed 19.5 knots. 868 passengers (154 first class, 714 tourist class).]

SYLVANIA.

The *Sylvania*, the last of this quartet and the last Cunarder to be designed for the North Atlantic trade only, arrived at New York for the first time in December 1957. In that same year *Newsweek* magazine ran a cover story that reported that, for the first time, the airlines were carrying more transatlantic passengers than the liner companies. But, in a burst of enthusiasm, it also reported that new ships such as the *Sylvania* would revive ocean-liner service on the Atlantic. This could not have been less accurate.

In winter, when the St. Lawrence was ice-clogged, these Canadian Cunarders ran to New York, calling at Halifax in each direction. In doing so, they offered what must have been some of Cunard's shortest sea voyages: two days to or from Halifax and for $20 in tourist class. [Built by John Brown & Company Limited, Clydebank, Scotland, 1957. 21,989 gross tons; 608 feet long; 80 feet wide. Steam turbines, twin screw. Service speed 19.5 knots. 878 passengers (154 first class, 724 tourist class).]

SAXONIA AND CARINTHIA.

The *Saxonia* and the *Ivernia* of 1954–55 were intended to be modern ships in every respect. Even their decor, here seen in the *Saxonia*'s tourist-class dining room *(above, bottom)*, was different—lighter and softer, more spacious looking and with less of the glossy, dark woods that Cunard designers and decorators had loved so. But to loyal passengers—and there were still legions of them—this new team of sisters was considered too modern. Some even critically called them "flashy." Many felt that Cunard had gone too far to please the passengers in tourist class. Dismayed and worried, Cunard reacted by revising the decor of the next set, the otherwise identical-looking *Carinthia* (of which the first-class lounge is shown above, top) and *Sylvania* of 1956–57. Their interiors reverted to a darker, heavier and more classical style. The chairs in the *Carinthia*'s first-class restaurant, for example, had been on board the *Aquitania* as far back as 1914.

CONVERSIONS TO CRUISING.

The new Canadian quartet began to lose passengers and cargo by the early sixties. In hindsight, it is regrettable that Cunard had not equipped them from the start for winter cruising. They did not have outdoor pools or extensive open deck spaces and most of their cabins were in the old transatlantic fashion, lacking private bathrooms. As the situation grew worse and passenger figures dropped, Cunard finally turned to the John Brown shipyards once again and asked them to convert the *Saxonia* and *Ivernia* for part-time tropical cruising. The entire transformation was also a test for the big, new transatlantic superliner that Cunard was then planning, which, with revisions, later became the *Queen Elizabeth 2*. These smaller Cunarders were given an entirely new look: redone public rooms, plumbing in all cabins and, perhaps most notable, the elimination of the aft cargo space, which was converted to a lido deck with verandas, umbrellas, lounge chairs and a kidney-shaped swimming pool (seen on the *Carmania*, formerly the *Saxonia*, *opposite, top*). These ships could now spend at least half the year in far more lucrative cruising, carrying Americans to the Caribbean. The ships were given new identities. The *Saxonia* became the *Carmania*, the *Ivernia* changed to *Franconia*. At first, they were even painted entirely in green as a reminder of the legendary *Caronia*, but were later repainted white. Eventually both cruised full-time. While the *Carmania* ran seasonal cruises from Southampton, the *Franconia* was, from 1967 until 1971, in regular weekly service between New York and Bermuda. She is shown above at Hamilton.

In the fall of 1967, the *Carinthia* closed out the Canadian service altogether and soon she and the *Sylvania* were sold. They were bought by the Sitmar Line and became the cruise ships *Fairsea* and *Fairwind* respectively. The *Carmania* and *Franconia* followed not too long afterward. Withdrawn by Cunard in 1971, they were sold two years later to the Soviets, becoming the *Leonid Sobinov* and *Feodor Shalyapin* respectively. These were Cunard's last traditional North Atlantic liners.

In the mid-sixties, Cunard, swept up by enthusiasm for the expanding cruise market, felt that even the aging *Queen Elizabeth* could be restyled for the trade. The *Elizabeth* had been the first of the Queens in the cruising trade, having made a five-day run from New York to Nassau and back in February 1963, with rates starting at $125. The *Mary* made her first cruise, from Southampton to Las Palmas in the Canaries, the following December.

In 1966, Cunard decided to spend £1 million on the renewal of the 26-year-old *Elizabeth*. Having been handed back to her builders in Scotland, she emerged with lounges redone, much more plumbing in her staterooms and a large pool deck built aft. A new addition was the Midships Bar (*opposite, bottom*). Generally, the decor was "hotel-at-the-airport," which clashed with the ship's older, more staid styling. Other rooms were altered by the addition of strings of colored lights, plastic flowers and decorations of corrugated paper. Cunard devotees disapproved. On one "gala" trip, the "Indian Summer Cruise" to the Mediterranean, the restyled *Elizabeth* carried fewer than 600 passengers. Cruise travelers, particularly in the United States, required a new breed of ship—one designed specifically as a cruise ship, a new, white, wedding cake of a vessel with discos and saunas, festive lounges and glitzy casinos. The Queens, well into middle age and just about museum pieces, had seen their best days.

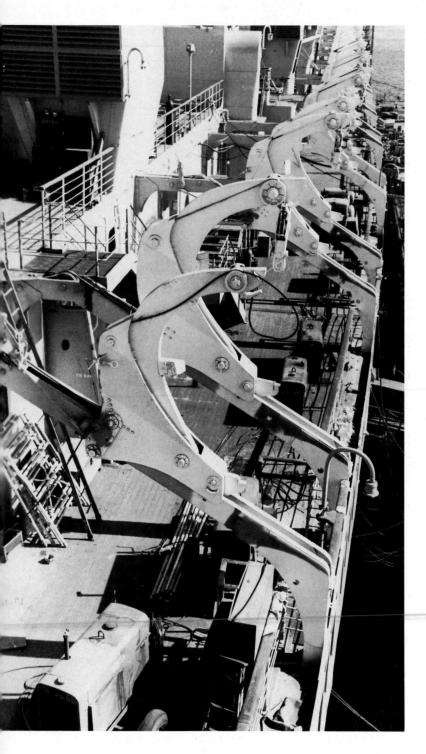

RETIRING THE *QUEEN MARY*.

May 9, 1967 was one of the most dramatic days in Cunard's peacetime history. The curtain was finally coming down: A message was flashed to the commanders of both Queens that the ships soon would be no more. The *Mary* would go that September; the *Elizabeth* in October 1968. The *Caronia*, the *Carinthia* and the *Sylvania* were also to be retired. Thereafter, the great Cunard Line would have only three liners—the *Carmania*, the *Franconia* and the supership then building on the Clyde.

The *Queen Mary* left New York for the last time on September 22 (*opposite, top*). There was enormous interest, for no ship better symbolized the glamour of the transatlantic era—and now its demise. She had been the most successful of all superliners, the most majestic Cunarder still in service, a ship heroic in war and perhaps the grandest and best loved in all of Cunard's history. Tugs, ferries and yachts escorted her downriver. Helicopters buzzed overhead and newspapers, television and radio widely reported on this "last farewell." She was leaving behind a splendid record: 1,000 crossings, 3.7 million miles, two million passengers and revenues of some $600 million in her 31 years. But now she was out of place, an anachronism in the new jet age.

In this view, the *Queen Mary*—the last three-stacker—passes the skyline of lower Manhattan for the last time. Workers in office buildings, accustomed to seeing the great ships come and go, made special note on this day. Ironically, that same week, demolition was started on the 47-story Singer Building (left of the *Mary*'s stern), the world's tallest when built in 1907. Making way for a far larger glass-and-steel tower, the Singer attained one last distinction: the tallest building yet razed.

Cunard had received a variety of proposals for the *Queen Mary* at the time of her retirement. Some investors wanted to make her into the world's largest immigrant ship, sailing from England out to Australia by way of the South African Cape, others planned to make her into a hotel and casino at Gibraltar, and New York City's Board of Education wanted to transform her into a floating high school stationed at the Brooklyn waterfront. Inevitably, Japanese scrap merchants also looked her over and made the highest bid Cunard had received—about $3.25 million. But an unlikely candidate won out in the end. The city of Long Beach, California, wanted her as a tourist attraction and bought her with a bid of $3.45 million. The great Atlantic liner would go into retirement on the Pacific.

The *Queen Mary* was chartered to a New York travel agency for one last sentimental journey: a long cruise from Southampton, around South America and up to Los Angeles. Lasting 40 days, it was the longest commercial trip she ever made. She reached that West Coast port on December 9, 1967, and two days later was officially removed from the British register of ships; the *Queen Mary* was now American. She underwent over three years of exhaustive refitting and renewing. A view of the boat deck (*left*), was taken during rehabilitation on August 21, 1970, when the lifeboats were still on shore. She emerged as the Hotel Queen Mary (opposite, bottom). Technically a building, since her propulsion systems had been removed, she was thought to be the ideal tourist complex—a hotel as well as a museum, shopping center and convention site. The entire make-over, which included the replacement of the original stacks with identical aluminum copies, cost a staggering $72 million—three times more than she had cost to be built 30 years before.

In May 1971, she opened to mixed reviews. Some buffs were delighted that she had been preserved, others were horrified by such touches as the hamburger stands on the promenade deck. Her success has been varied and there have been times when the Japanese scrappers have taken another look at her.

The *Queen Mary* has been joined at Long Beach by another engineering wonder, Howard Hughes's flying boat *Spruce Goose*. At present, both are under the management of the Walt Disney Corporation. Still more millions have been poured into the *Queen Mary* to sharpen her appeal to tourists. Now, some 60 years after her first keel plates were laid, she seems reassured of a long future. The most successful of all Atlantic superships, a Blue Ribbon champion, a gallant wartime trooper, the last three-stacker, a ship of glamour and style, she stands as a monument to a grand age.

THE END OF THE *QUEEN ELIZABETH.*

Despite the increasing inroads made by the airlines and the loss of seagoing passengers, it had been thought that the *Queen Elizabeth* would remain in service until as late as 1975, serving as the companion to the new Queen then being built on the Clyde. The idea was unrealistic, for the aged *Elizabeth* could not have been paired successfully with a brand-new, sparkling liner–cruise ship. Furthermore, it was doubtful that Cunard could still maintain two large liners on a weekly transatlantic shuttle into the seventies. And so, in October 1968, the 28-year-old *Elizabeth* was retired. Dressed in flags and flying a "paying off" (ending service) pennant from her aft mast, the *Queen Elizabeth*, the world's largest ocean liner, left New York for the last time *(opposite).* When sunlight filtered through the threatening clouds, the ship glowed, but also revealed traces of these hard times for the dwindling Cunard fleet. Parts of her once immaculate hull and upperworks were scarred by rust, often great streaks of it.

It had been intended to make the retired *Queen Elizabeth* the American East Coast version of the *Mary.* In December 1968, she was sent to Port Everglades, Florida. There she was to be transformed into a hotel, shopping mall, museum and convention center. Optimistically, Cunard even retained an 85 percent share in the project. Nothing came to pass except mismanagement, scandals and court battles. The *Elizabeth* sat idle, rusting in the Florida sun. The Japanese scrap dealers were again on the scene. Late in the summer of 1970, however, Taiwanese shipping tycoon C. Y. Tung bought her for restoration and conversion into a combination cruise ship–floating university. Renamed *Seawise University,* she was sent to Hong Kong for extensive alterations. On the back of this photograph of 1971 *(left),* journalist James L. Shaw noted, "Conversion work on the *Seawise University* was carried out quickly at Hong Kong, but decks were left a shambles in the process."

On January 9, 1972, nearing the very end of her renewal, she caught fire (five separate fires on the same day) and turned into a blistering inferno *(above).* Overloaded with firefighters' water, she capsized the next day. Arson has never been ruled out. The Japanese scrappers again reappeared, and this time they won the contract and cut up her remains. By 1974, the former *Queen Elizabeth* was gone from Hong Kong harbor, a tragic ending for an outstanding ship.

LAST DAYS OF THE *CARONIA*.

The legendary *Caronia* faced hard times in the end as well. Surpassed by a new generation of luxury cruise ships represented by such vessels as the *Kungsholm* and the *Sagafjord*, she was retired soon after the *Queen Mary*. After being sold to Greek interests, operating under the Panamanian flag, who had renamed her *Caribia*, she endured the longest twilight of any Cunarder. She was barely back in service, in February 1969, when she was damaged by fire in the Caribbean and had to be towed all the way back to New York. For the next years, she remained there, loitering about the harbor—at shipyards, old Brooklyn cargo docks, anchorages, the unused United States Lines passenger terminal (where she is shown here) and finally the near-derelict Pier 56, formerly used by Cunard for the likes of the old *Aquitania* and *Berengaria*. None of the frequent rumors of her renovation came to pass. Faded, rusting and lifeless, the ship slipped further and further into decay. There were lawsuits, crew defections, problems with harbor authorities and even a "parking ticket" for being docked illegally. Finally, in the winter of 1974, she was sold for scrap. Her littered decks, musty ballrooms and darkened staterooms were opened to the public for a nostalgic auction, a chance to buy pieces of the grand ocean-liner era. Everything was tagged, from sofas and coffee tables to telephones and battered saucepans from the kitchens. The ship was all but completely stripped. In the end, en route to the scrappers on Taiwan, the former *Caronia* was lost. Seeking safe waters from a tropical storm at Guam, she was thrown onto a local breakwater and broke in three. Her wreckage was a menace to shipping and the remains were quickly cut up.

THE CRUISE AGE: THE QE2 AND THE CONTEMPORARY CUNARDERS

IN MAY 1969, ON an overcast day, New York harbor put on what was almost certainly its final gala reception for a transatlantic superliner. Flag-bedecked tugs and spraying fireboats, sumptuous yachts and specially chartered excursion craft formed a welcoming flotilla. Everyone was excited, awaiting the first glimpse of the new ship when it appeared beyond the Verrazano-Narrows Bridge. The majesty and stateliness of the the old Queens were still fresh in memory—the criteria of what big ocean liners were supposed to look like. But this new arrival revealed something close to a complete change. The new *Queen Elizabeth 2*, the last of the transatlantic breed, the very biggest liner ever intended for a schedule of crossings and cruises, was the ship that represented the "new," trendier Cunard.

Cunard had done some serious rethinking during the sixties. Traditional designs for a replacement for both Queens were discarded. The days of a full-time Atlantic liner were over. Instead, this new giant had to be much more of a floating hotel, a fast, large "moving resort" that, having effectively and efficiently relayed its guests across the North Atlantic, could, with very few changes made within a few hours, sail off to the tropics as a cruise ship. On cruises, passengers enjoyed a seagoing vacation in which the ports were diversions, not destinations.

And so, when she first appeared in the Lower Bay on that May morning, the *QE2* was indeed a radical departure from her predecessors. Her single pipelike stack proclaimed the differences. The new generation of sales and marketing people at Cunard felt that she should be a complete break with the Cunard of the past. So, instead of the ornately columned lounges and the dark wood panels, the triple classes, the mood of an older, almost lost, world, there would be a sleek, flashy resort with discos and casinos, top-deck lidos and shopping arcades and after-dinner revues of befeathered dancing girls. Even the traditional Cunard colors on her funnel were gone and the name Cunard was painted in orange-red lettering on the superstructure near the bridge wings. She looked every inch the floating hotel.

The *Queen Elizabeth 2* has won praise, has garnered enormous publicity and has had considerable popularity ever since. She remains the flagship, but of a far different Cunard, a company now part of the huge Trafalgar House Group, based at Southampton instead of Liverpool, housed in New York in far less splendid surroundings than in earlier years and a firm that is more of a travel-and-leisure business than steamship company. The accountants seem to rule nowadays. Cunard's seven liners (only two of which are registered under the British flag, which is expensive) are run to be most efficient, sailing on routes all over the world, and to carry the most passengers at the highest profit. The *QE2* still runs her sunshine cruises and Atlantic crossings. The opulent *Sagafjord* and *Vistafjord*, acquired from the Norwegians, travel almost everywhere. Far-ranging itineraries are also given to the twin luxury cruise yachts, the *Sea Goddess I* and *Sea Goddess II*, also former Norwegians. Finally, the company has the *Cunard Countess*, based in the ever-popular Caribbean, and her sister, the *Cunard Princess*, which sails almost entirely in Mediterranean waters.

Cunard has kept pace in the multibillion-dollar international-cruise industry. Although it is no longer the biggest liner firm, it remains a major force in the industry. While so many of its earlier competitors and contemporaries have disappeared completely, Cunard survives and endures, having attained 150 years of glorious service. And what of the future? There are frequent rumors of additional tonnage and even a joint cruise project with the affluent Japanese. We feel sure that there will be other Cunarders to add to our list and that there will be much more to be written about the great Cunard Line.

TWILIGHT OF THE TRANSATLANTIC LINERS.
The days of the Atlantic fleet were ending. This photograph was taken on a murky afternoon in February 1973, as three of the four remaining transatlantic superliners were in port together. Italy's *Michelangelo* is to the left, the *Queen Elizabeth 2* (whose story follows) is in center and the *France* on the right. Late in 1969, the last of the Blue Ribbon champions, the *United States,* had been decommissioned. In the face of continually declining passenger loads and staggering operational costs, the *France* would go as well, in 1974, and the two big Italians (the *Raffaello* being the other) would be gone by the following year. Thereafter, the *QE2* sailed alone, the last Atlantic greyhound. There were rumors that she was deficit-ridden, a burden to both the British government and Cunard, and that she might even be at the scrappers by her tenth birthday. Happily, there were enough liner enthusiasts and others who wanted to experience at least one crossing to ensure her financial support. In fact, by the mid-1980s, she actually carried more passengers and earned greater profits than ever before. Cunard's gamble to build her had paid off.

QUEEN ELIZABETH 2.

To build its new supership, Cunard again turned to the John Brown yards on the Clyde. In the early 1960s, a project designated "Q3" was on the boards—a design for a traditional, three-class liner that would run all year on the Atlantic. But it quickly became apparent that the plan had been a miscalculation; by 1965, the airlines handled 95 percent of all transatlantic travel. The designs for the ship were reworked. As a two-class liner that could easily be converted to one-class for cruising, she would be filled with an abundance of contemporary facilities—a movie theater, lavish lounges, lidos, colorful discos—plying the transatlantic service for only half the year.

The first keel plates were laid on June 5, 1965. As had the *Queen Mary*, which occupied the same slipway 30 years before, the new ship remained nameless until launching day, being known as John Brown Number 736 (*opposite, bottom left*).

Naming the new Cunarder was a problem in itself. While under construction, Cunard had dubbed her "Q4." At its new streamlined Southampton headquarters, Cunard management wanted lots of change—the ship was to represent "new Britain" (especially a Britain that was welcoming more and more American tourists). The company considered names that were less in the Cunard tradition, sounding more like good British hotels—Great Britain, William Shakespeare, Winston Churchill and London are said to have been mentioned. Traditionalists suggested such names as Britannia, Mauretania and Queen Mary II. But it was left to Queen Elizabeth herself, who, like her grandmother in 1934 and her mother in 1938, consented to name the liner at her launching. And so, on September 20, 1967, using the same pair of golden scissors that had released the christening champagne on the previous Queens, Queen Elizabeth named the new Cunarder *Queen Elizabeth 2*, honoring the original *Queen Elizabeth* (not, as many had thought, the Queen herself). Evidently, it had been decided to let the name *Queen Mary* remain with the majestic old three-stacker that was soon to go off to permanent retirement in southern California. The new liner was popularly known as the *QE2*.

The ship's maiden voyage, orginally set for January 1969, was put off until May, following a series of mechanical problems and Cunard's refusals to accept her. She left Southampton on May 2, and five days later reached New York for a gala reception (*opposite, top*). In this view, five Moran tugs are on the port side, giving what journalists then called the "royal push." Dressed in flags and floodlit by night,

she was berthed at Pier 92, the same slip that had been used by the previous Queens and the *Mauretania*, the *Caronia*, the *Britannic* and others. Hail to the Queen! She was their successor.

The *QE2* has become synonymous with seagoing luxury. On her winter around-the-world cruises, which began in 1975, there was an increased demand for deluxe, higher-priced accommodations. And so, in December 1978, while undergoing her annual overhaul at the large Bayonne graving dock in New York harbor, several prefabricated suites were placed on board (*opposite, bottom right*). Some appraised them as the most lavish shipboard quarters of their time. A 149-day circumnavigation on the *Carinthia* had been priced from $2000 (including all shore excursions) in 1926; fares on the *QE2* for 95 days began at $15,000 in 1986 (with additional fees being paid for excursions).

Having received enormous publicity over the years, the *QE2* is probably the most celebrated liner of her time. There have been disruptive strikes, hurricanes and even the plot of a submarine attack in the eastern Mediterranean. But her greatest publicity surely must have come in May 1982, when she was suddenly called to duty as a troopship in Britain's conflict with Argentina over the Falkland Islands. Cunard could never have guessed that its third Queen would serve a military function as had her predecessors in carrying military passengers. Chartered by the Ministry of War Transport at $225,000 a day, she took 3,000 troops from Southampton to the troubled Falklands, where she had to be especially careful since, from all reports, the Argentines were keen on sinking her. She survived and returned to a heroic welcome at Southampton. In this view, in August of the same year, she has just been restored and is about to return to North Atlantic service. The battle-scarred P&O liner *Canberra* is to the left, awaiting her own restoration following even more extensive service.

Fresh out of the old King George V Graving Dock (*above*) the *QE2* is sporting a new look: a dove-gray hull and the first appearance of the traditional Cunard orange-red colors on her funnel. However, the gray proved impractical and she reverted to charcoal-black. [Built by John Brown & Company Limited (later renamed Upper Clyde Shipbuilders, Limited), Clydebank, Scotland, 1965–68. 65,863 gross tons; 963 feet long; 105 feet wide; 32-foot draft. Steam turbines, twin screw. Service speed 28.5 knots. 2,005 passengers (564 first class, 1,441 tourist class).]

The QE2. The turn-of-the-century practice of making first-class quarters resemble shoreside accommodations still holds true aboard the *QE2*. Once the drapes are drawn and the views of the sea hidden, you might well be in a top-class hotel on shore. The Queen's Room *(right, top)*, one of the loveliest on board, is used for afternoon teas, lectures, demonstrations and evening cabaret.

Passengers in top-grade staterooms and suites are assigned to one of the two grill rooms, the smaller Princess Grill or the Queen's Grill *(right, middle)*. Many passengers have reported that their best shipboard dining experiences have been in these grill rooms.

The best accommodations on board *(right, bottom)* feature large living rooms, bedrooms, full baths and complete dressing and trunk rooms. Some even have private terraces. It would seem that every amenity is included, from bedside television controls and hair dryers to wall safes and fully stocked private bars.

The QE2. The *QE2*'s turbines proved troublesome, often making it difficult for her to maintain her schedule. As her years advanced, there seemed to be more frequent breakdowns and other mechanical woes. Cunard decided that she would undergo the huge conversion from steam turbine to diesel-electric. With British yards unable to compete, a West German shipyard at Bremerhaven won the prized contract worth $162 million (or more than twice what the ship had cost to build). In the preliminary analysis, Cunard had estimated that a complete replacement of similar size, speed and capacity could cost as much as $400 million (or five times the *QE2*'s cost in the late sixties).

In October 1987, the *QE2* established yet another record: She made the last regular Atlantic passage under steam. When she returned the following May, with a new look that included a redesigned funnel, the dieselized Queen was more efficient and faster than before. By 1990, with her summer schedule of five-day crossings, she was running the fastest turnaround schedule in the history of transatlantic shipping.

The *QE2*'s transatlantic popularity has remained intact primarily because of Cunard's clever and effective sales and marketing. She is the cruise ship that makes the last Atlantic passages. Combined with her crossings are a seemingly endless variety of tour and travel packages: one way by sea and the other by air, *QE2* and the supersonic Concorde, *QE2* and motor tours of Britain, a selection of European tours and even one that includes the fabled Orient Express. The *QE2* remains one of the greatest travel experiences.

CUNARD ADVENTURER (above).

By the late 1960s, Cunard seemed undecided about its future path. Cruising was clearly the new mainstay, but the company was unsure precisely what type and size of passenger vessel to build. It bought a 50 percent share in a new cruise project being organized by Overseas National Airways, a charter airline. Built in a Dutch shipyard, the two new ships were of a practical design—efficient, smaller, easy to navigate in even the most remote cruise ports. When Overseas National encountered financial problems, Cunard bought the uncompleted pair outright and named them the *Cunard Adventurer* and the *Cunard Ambassador*. Completed in 1971-72, they had a slight resemblance to the *QE2*. They were used in the Caribbean.

The Cunard careers of these ships were quite short. The *Cunard Ambassador* burned in September 1974 and was so badly damaged that she was sold, being rebuilt as a Danish sheep carrier. In 1984, after another fire, she went to Taiwanese ship breakers. In late 1976, the *Cunard Adventurer* was sold to the Norwegian Caribbean Lines, which still sails her as their *Sunward II*. [*Cunard Adventurer*: Built by Rotterdam Dry Dock Company, Rotterdam, the Netherlands. 14,155 gross tons; 484 feet long; 71 feet wide. Diesels, twin screw. Service speed 20.5 knots. 806 first-class passengers.]

CUNARD COUNTESS (opposite, top).

To replace the *Cunard Adventurer* and *Cunard Ambassador*, the company added two larger, improved versions that were initially intended to be a part of an eight-ship series being planned by MGM, the Hollywood film company that had become interested in diversification. Although the scheme never materialized, Cunard had the first two completed to its own specifications. Unique among passenger ships, they were constructed at a Copenhagen shipyard and towed to La Spezia, in Italy, for outfitting and final delivery. They were completed as the *Cunard Countess* (summer 1976) and the *Cunard Princess* (spring 1977). Compact and ideally suited to the one- and two-week "fly 'n' sail" business, this team is to the present Cunard fleet what the A class intermediate liners were to the North Atlantic trade in the twenties and thirties.

The *Cunard Countess* serves full-time in the Caribbean, working alternating seven-day itineraries out of San Juan. One week she travels to Tortola, St. Maarten, Guadeloupe, St. Lucia, Antigua and St. Thomas; the other to Grenada, Trinidad, Barbados, Martinique and St. Thomas. After stints in the Caribbean, as well as cruises to Alaska, Mexico and Bermuda, the *Cunard Princess* has been reassigned to European service, cruising to such Mediterranean ports as Málaga, Venice, Dubrovnik, Mykonos, Alexandria and Istanbul. [*Cunard Countess*: Built by Burmeister & Wain Shipyards, Copenhagen, Denmark; completed by Industrie Navali Mechaniche Affine Shipyard, La Spezia, Italy, 1976. 17,495 gross tons; 536 feet long; 74 feet wide. B&W-type diesels, twin screw. Service speed 20.5 knots. 750 cruise passengers.]

SAGAFJORD (opposite, bottom).

The 1980s were a decade of acquisitions for Cunard. After studying plans for building new tonnage, in 1983 the company opted instead to buy the impeccable Norwegian America Line's *Sagafjord* and *Vistafjord*, both among the highest-rated cruise ships. They were ideally suited to follow in the wake of the legendary *Caronia*.

Both the Bahamian-registered *Sagafjord* and *Vistafjord* are like big yachts, having the feeling of a floating country club, with 500 passengers being looked after by 350 crew. To please its demanding clientele (including guests who remain on board for voyage after voyage), Cunard often changes the itineraries of these liners. In 1990, for example, during Cunard's anniversary celebrations, the *Sagafjord* cruised around the world for 97 days, made several Caribbean and trans-Panama Canal trips, spent the summer in Alaskan waters (where she is shown at Juneau) and then went to Hawaii, Australia and the South Sea islands for much of the autumn. Having started her year on a five-continent cruise that included South America, Africa and India, the *Vistafjord* spent the spring roaming the Mediterranean and Black Seas. In summer, she cruised out of Hamburg to Scandinavia, the Baltic cities and even up to Spitzbergen. That July, she made a special hundred-fiftieth-anniversary cruise, calling at Amsterdam, Zeebrugge (Belgium), Plymouth, Cobh, Milford Haven, a special fleet review at Spithead in honor of Cunard, then Southampton, London, Edinburgh, Kirkwall and Lerwick, before returning to Hamburg. She returned to the Mediterranean in the fall only to cross to the Caribbean and Florida by the end of the year. [*Sagafjord*: Built by Société des Forges et Chantiers de la Mediterranée, Toulon, France, 1965. 24,002 gross tons; 615 feet long; 82 feet wide. Sulzer diesels, twin screw. Service speed 20 knots. 789 cruise passengers.]

SEA GODDESS I AND SEA GODDESS II.

The *Sea Goddess I* and *Sea Goddess II*, owned by Sea Goddess Cruises, a Norwegian firm, were completed in 1984–85 as the ultimate cruise yachts. Carrying a maximum of 116 passengers, they represented yet another dimension to the ever-expanding cruise industry: a select, personalized ambience combined with visits to unique, often remote ports of call. A sample itinerary would be 11 days in the Mediterranean, sailing from Monte Carlo (where both ships are seen here; *Sea Goddess I* berthed to the right and *Sea Goddess II* to the left) to call at Sorrento, Capri, Bonifacio, Ibiza, Barcelona, Collura, St. Tropez and Portofino before returning to Monte Carlo. Minimum fares, the highest in the world at the time (1986), began at $6,900 (or $627 a day).

They have been called "the most luxurious passenger ships ever to sail." Every cabin, for example, has a full sitting room that can be easily converted to a private dining room. Each stateroom has its own library, stereo system, television and video systems, spacious closets, caviar- and salmon-filled refrigerator and a bar stocked with guests' favorite drinks. Amenities include a health center, outdoor pool, beauty salon, casino, gift shop, outdoor café (for breakfasts and lunches), several bars and a main salon. Unique is the stern "tailgate" platform that can be lowered for easy access to the sea for swimming, waterskiing, windsurfing and snorkeling. All necessary equipment, including sailboats and twin speedboats, is provided. The aft part of the funnel serves as a decorative waterfall. All wines and champagnes are included in the fares and all meals are cooked to order. Passengers can dine whenever they wish, either in the main restaurant or in their staterooms.

When Sea Goddess Cruises encountered financial difficulties and both ships were about to be repossessed by their Finnish builders, Cunard cleverly arranged for a 12-year charter of the pair in the summer of 1986. The operation became Cunard–Sea Goddess Cruises and the ships wear Cunard funnel colors.

In 1990, its celebratory year, Cunard remains a grand name as owner of the last Atlantic superliner, four of the highest-rated, most luxurious cruise ships afloat and two other important cruise ships. The tradition continues. [Built by Wärtsilä Shipyards, Helsinki, Finland, 1984–85. 4,200 gross tons; 344 feet long; 58 feet wide. Diesels, twin screw. Service speed 18 knots. 116 first-class passengers.]

BIBLIOGRAPHY

Bonsor, N. R. P. *North Atlantic Seaway.* Prescot, Lancashire: T. Stephenson & Sons, Limited, 1955.

Braynard, Frank O. *Lives of the Liners.* New York: Cornell Maritime Press, Inc., 1947.

Braynard, Frank O. *The World's Greatest Ship—S.S. Leviathan,* 6 vols. Privately published, 1972–83 (available from the author).

Braynard, Frank O., & Miller, William H. *Fifty Famous Liners,* 3 vols. Wellingborough, Northamptonshire: Patrick Stephens, Limited, 1982–88.

Brinnin, John Malcom, & Gaulin, Kenneth. *Grand Luxe: The Transatlantic Style.* New York: Henry Holt & Company, 1988.

Coleman, Terry. *The Liners.* New York: G. P. Putnam's Sons, 1977.

de Kerbrech, Richard, & Williams, David L. *Cunard–White Star Liners of the 1930s.* London: Conway Maritime Press, Limited, 1988.

Dodman, Frank E. *Ships of the Cunard Line.* London: Adlard Coles, Limited, 1955.

Dunn, Laurence. *Passenger Liners.* Southampton: Adlard Coles, Limited, 1961.

Horton White, A. G. *Ships of the North Atlantic.* London: Sampson Low, Marston & Company, Limited, 1937.

Hutchings, David F. *Queen Elizabeth: From Victory to Valhalla.* Southampton: Kingfisher Productions, 1990.

Hutchings, David F. *Queen Elizabeth 2: A Ship for all Seasons.* Southampton: Kingfisher Productions, 1988.

Hutchings, David F. *Queen Mary: 50 Years of Splendour.* Southampton: Kingfisher Productions, 1986.

Hutchings, David F. *Titanic: 75 Years of Legend.* Southampton: Kingfisher Productions, 1987.

Hyde, Francis E. *Cunard and the North Atlantic 1840–1973.* London: The Macmillan Press, Limited, 1975.

Johnson, Howard. *The Cunard Story.* London: Whittet Books, Limited, 1987.

Kludas, Arnold. *Great Passenger Ships of the World,* 5 vols. Cambridge, England: Patrick Stephens, Limited, 1972–76.

Lacey, Robert. *Queens of the North Atlantic.* London: Sidgwick & Jackson, Limited, 1973.

MacLean, Donald. *Queen's Company.* London: Hutchinson & Company, Limited, 1965.

Maxtone-Graham, John. *Cunard: 150 Glorious Years.* Newton Abbot, Devon: David & Charles, Limited, 1989.

Maxtone-Graham, John. *Liners To The Sun.* New York: The Macmillan Company, 1985.

Maxtone-Graham, John. *The Only Way To Cross.* New York: The Macmillan Company, 1972.

Miller, William H. *British Ocean Liners: A Twilight Era, 1960–85.* Wellingborough, Northamptonshire: Patrick Stephens, Limited, 1986.

Miller, William H. *The Cruiseships.* Wellingborough, Northamptonshire: Patrick Stephens, Limited, 1988.

Miller, William H., Jr. *The Great Luxury Liners, 1927–54: A Photographic Record.* New York: Dover Publications, Inc., 1981.

Miller, William H., Jr. *The Last Atlantic Liners.* London: Conway Maritime Press, Limited, 1985.

Miller, William H., Jr. *Transatlantic Liners, 1945–80.* Newton Abbot, Devon: David & Charles, Limited, 1981.

Miller, William H., & Hutchings, David F. *Transatlantic Liners at War: The Story of the Queens.* Newton Abbot, Devon: David & Charles, Limited, 1985.

Mitchell, W. H. *The Cunard Line: A Post-War History.* Deal, Kent: Marinart, Limited, 1975.

Potter, Neil, & Frost, Jack. *The Elizabeth.* London: George G. Harrap & Company, Limited, 1965.

Potter, Neil, & Frost, Jack. *The Mary, The Inevitable Ship.* London: George G. Harrap & Company, Limited, 1961.

Stevens, Leonard A. *The Elizabeth: The Passage of a Queen.* New York: Alfred A. Knopf, 1968.

INDEX OF SHIPS ILLUSTRATED

The pages listed are those containing text references.